Copenhagen became the capital of Denmark fifty years before discovery of America! Rio de Janeiro and Sugar Loaf are seen spectacularly from the top of Corcovado. Heron Castle, symbolizing ancient Japan, stands near Himeji. (Photos: Konstantin Kostich; Hagopian—Shostal; McKeon—FPG)

AROUND THE WORLD
IN 1,000 PICTURES

Braniff Super Convair 340

Matson Lines Lurline

Sabena Belgian Air Line

Italian Line Cristoforo Colombo

United States welcomed to New York—United States Lines

TWA Constellation

Holland-America Nieuw Amsterdam

French Railroads "Blue Train"

American Export Lines Indep

Swissair DC-6B

Canadian Pacific Empress of Scotland

Scandinavian Airlines System

Furness Queen of Bermuda

Air France Constellations

French Line Ile de Fran

AROUND THE
WORLD
IN 1,000 PICTURES

A PHOTOGRAPHIC ENCYCLOPEDIA
OF TRAVEL TO FOREIGN LANDS

Edited by A. MILTON RUNYON
and VILMA F. BERGANE

FOREWORD BY RICHARD JOSEPH
10 MAPS BY RAFAEL PALACIOS

DOUBLEDAY & COMPANY, INC.
Garden City, N.Y.

Pan American "Clipper"

Europabus

Swedish American Line Kungsholm

Grace Line Santa Rosa

Trans-Canada "Viscount"

Cunard Line Caronia

FOR LAURA

CONTENTS

Foreword 7

VOYAGE 1
Bermuda and the Caribbean . 9
  Bermuda 11
  Cuba 18
  Nassau 24
  Jamaica 29
  Haiti 33
  Dominican Republic . . . 36
  Puerto Rico 39
  Martinique 43
  Guadeloupe 45
  Antigua 46
  Virgin Islands 47
  Trinidad 51
  Tobago 54
  Netherlands West Indies . . 55
  Barbados 60
  Grenada 62
  St. Lucia 64

VOYAGE 2
Canada and Alaska . . . 65
  Quebec City 67
  Quebec 70
  Montreal 73
  Nova Scotia 75
  New Brunswick . . . 76
  Prince Edward Island . . 77

  Newfoundland 78
  Ontario 79
  Manitoba 83
  Saskatchewan 84
  Alberta 85
  British Columbia . . . 92
  Alaska 94

VOYAGE 3
Mexico and Central America . 97
  Mexico 99
  Guatemala 117
  El Salvador 120
  Honduras 121
  Nicaragua 122
  Panama Canal 124
  Panama 126
  Costa Rica 128

VOYAGE 4
South America 129
  Venezuela 131
  Brazil 136
  Uruguay 141
  Argentina 144
  Paraguay 148
  Chile 149
  Bolivia 153
  Peru 156
  Colombia 158
  Ecuador 160

VOYAGE 5
Great Britain and Ireland . . 161
London 163
England 176
Scotland 199
Wales 207
Northern Ireland . . . 211
Ireland 215

VOYAGE 6
Scandinavia 225
Norway 227
Sweden 234
Finland 241
Denmark 247
Iceland 256

VOYAGE 7
Europe 257
The Netherlands 259
Belgium 267
Luxembourg 275
Paris 277
France 289
Monaco 302
Germany 303
Austria 308
Switzerland 311

VOYAGE 8
The Mediterranean 321
Portugal 323
Madeira and Azores . . . 327
Spain 328
Majorca and Canary Islands 338
Tunisia 339
Algeria 340
Morocco 342

Rome 343
Italy 352
Sicily 374
Greece 375
Yugoslavia 378
Israel 379
Turkey 382
Lebanon 384

VOYAGE 9
Round-the-World Cruise . . 385
Hawaii 387
Japan 393
Hong Kong 398
Philippines 400
Thailand 402
Java 404
Bali 405
Sumatra 406
Burma 407
Singapore 408
Ceylon 410
India 412
Kashmir 419
Pakistan 420
Egypt 421
British East Africa . . . 424
Rhodesia 426
South Africa 427

VOYAGE 10
South Pacific 431
Fiji 433
Australia 434
New Zealand 442
Tahiti 446
INDEX 447

FOREWORD
by Richard Joseph

In the catalog of man's dreams, taking a trip around the world ranks with making a million dollars, being elected President of the United States or inheriting a South Sea island. It's the ultimate travel experience, and next to it even the most fabulous junket fades into insignificance.

Like so many dreams, a world-tour can become a reality for only a comparatively few people, even though you can now fly around the world for about two thousand dollars, and one airline already is promoting round-the-world flights for the two-week vacationist. Nevertheless the odds are still strongly against your visiting most of the places covered in the following pages.

That being the case, this book is a working substitute for a trip around the world. The well-over-a-thousand pictures which follow will give you many of the sights and evoke some of the sounds, smells, tastes and moods of those far-away places with the fabulous names. They cover all the free world outside the continental United States which can be reached conveniently by American pleasure travelers. You'll sense some of the space of the far Pacific, see the breeze rustling the leaves of the palm trees on Waikiki, smell the

Mr. Joseph is Travel Editor of Esquire Magazine *and author of* WORLD WIDE TRAVEL GUIDE, YOUR TRIP TO BRITAIN, WORLD WIDE MONEY CONVERTER AND TIPPING GUIDE, *and with Muriel E. Richter,* WORLD WIDE TRAVEL REGULATIONS MADE EASY.

delicate fragrance of jasmine tea handed you in a fragile cup by a geisha girl in Kyoto. You will feel the life pulsating through the pack-jammed sampans in Hong Kong harbor, absorb the peace of a Buddhist shrine in Thailand, understand the loneliness of Africa's vast open places, and come back to the world you know in the street scenes of western Europe.

The photographs are arranged in a number of tours, following the same itineraries a traveler would take in seeing the world in a series of different trips. And they've been chosen to give you the best possible idea of what you'd actually see on your world travels rather than dealing with impossibly remote spots or esoteric subjects available to the correspondent and professional photographer but not to the average pleasure traveler.

That's why you'll see many pictures of ordinary people the world

7

over, but none of political leaders or celebrities of any sort. The photos will reveal to you the usual life of the various countries of the world; they won't take you for a weekend at the country home of an Indian Maharajah or English Viscount, backstage at a rehearsal of the *Folies Bergère* or between the spokes of a wheel in a tractor factory.

The things you'll see in these pictures, in other words, are the things you'd really see on a tour of the world. And the pictures are the same sort of pictures that can be and frequently are taken by the average traveler (I've been able to contribute quite a few myself), although they've been carefully selected for subject interest and photographic excellence. The editors have screened out the fuzzy prints, and the shots of Grandma with the doorman of the Grande Hotel; nevertheless you'll recognize photos of some of the places you've been to as duplicates of some of the better pictures you've taken yourself.

That, for me, is one of the charms of the book, the identification the traveler will feel for many of the pictures he'll see. This volume really has a three-fold attraction: it will give the intending traveler a preview of some of the fantastic things he'll see in various parts of the globe, it will treat the man who has been there to some wonderfully nostalgic memories of what he's seen and experienced, and it will give the armchair traveler a knowledge of the world and an intimate feeling of having been to most of the colorful places on earth.

There's a proverb, allegedly ancient Chinese, to the effect that *"The world is a book, and he who stays at home reads only one page."* Read all the pages of this book, though, and you will have seen the world.

Voyage 1
BERMUDA AND THE CARIBBEAN

The many islands, large and small, off the southeast coast of the United States have become most popular for both winter and summer vacations, because they give you "a trip abroad" with minimum time and with any sort of expenditure you wish to make.

There are dozens of cruises through the Caribbean, especially from December through March, many of them by transatlantic liners put on the job of earning dollars for their owners during the time when travel to the European ports is slack. Taking such a ship is a good way to "try out" a trip abroad and see how it appeals to you. Many of the cruises offer lavish entertainment, planned shore excursions.

There are also regularly scheduled trips throughout the year by such attractive vessels as Furness' *Queen of Bermuda* and new *Ocean Monarch*. They make frequent trips to Bermuda, with longer cruises from time to time. Easter and Christmas cruises are especially popular.

By air, almost any point in the West Indies is reached in a few hours. Pan American, BOAC, Eastern Airlines and others provide a network of air routes that will take you any particular place, or a combination of places, quickly and

"Ocean Monarch" docks at St. George's.

pleasantly. Bermuda is served by Pan American, BOAC and Colonial. The flight takes 3 to 4 hours, depending upon equipment and winds.

Variety is certainly offered by the enchanting isles of the West Indies. If you want gaiety, bustle and lots of entertainment, choose Havana, San Juan, or Kingston. For quietude in the dignity of British colonial atmosphere, you'll like Nassau and Bermuda and Montego Bay. For the real "far, far away from it all" effect, you'll want one of the Virgin Islands, or the barely discovered Antigua or St. Lucia.

One of the best things to do is to make a sort of survey trip the first time, by cruise ship or by air, and "sample" several places on one trip. Cruise itineraries and air excursions often enable you to visit several of the islands at no greater cost than visiting one. Then you can pick the spot you like the best for next time.

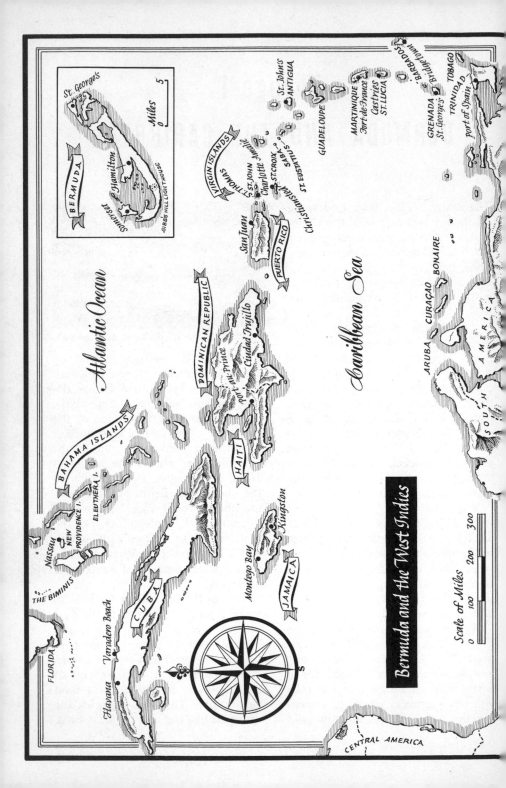

Bermuda and the West Indies

CAMBRIDGE BEACHES IN SOMERSET IS A TYPICAL COTTAGE COLONY.

LOVELY BERMUDA HAS PEACE, QUIET

"Tranquil and contenting" were Mark Twain's words for Bermuda, and thousands of visitors have found it so, even when horses and carriages have given way to motorbikes and small English autos. Gulf Stream protection prevents extremes of temperature. Easter lilies, oleander combine with pink sands and blue-green sea waters for real beauty.

11

Bermuda

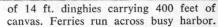

Hamilton Harbor is the home of Royal Bermuda Yacht Club, famous for racing of 14 ft. dinghies carrying 400 feet of canvas. Ferries run across busy harbor.

Surreys and drays have largely been replaced by Austins and Morris Minors.

Bicycles and Velos—bikes with motors on front wheel—are favorite transportation.

Photos: Bermuda News Bureau; bottom left, Lester L. Baker

Fields of Easter lilies are a lovely sight in the spring. They're shipped everywhere.

Bermuda homes are built of native stone, in white, or in pastel pink, blue, purple.

Grape Bay has one of the many secluded beaches. The sands, eroded from coral rock, are often pink in color. The water sparkles in brilliant greens and blues.

Bermuda

Par-le-Ville Gardens, on Queen Street next to library, make a pleasant place to rest after a trip to Hamilton's many shops where you get fine British woolens.

Front Street, Hamilton, usually bustling, is very peaceful when shops are closed.

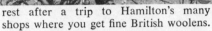

Crystal Caves, Leamington Caves offer stalactites and stalagmites, and souvenirs.

SWIZZLE INN IS FAVORITE STOP.

WORLD'S TINIEST DRAW BRIDGE.

14

Bermuda Cathedral stands at a high point, is one of islands' many churches.

The Devil's Hole, a natural aquarium, is place where you can fish without hooks.

Gibb's Hill Light House affords a view from its top of many of the 150 islands.

This "Moon Gate" is one of several, an odd design said to be copied from China.

S.S. QUEEN OF BERMUDA DOCKS RIGHT AT FRONT STREET, HAMILTON

Photos: Bermuda News Bureau; top right, center left, A. Milton Runyon

Bermuda

The Reefs Beach Club is a picturesque cabana colony built on the rugged coral cliffs of the south shore overlooking Christian Bay. At left is Gibb's Hill.

Your carriage waits right at the dock where the *Queen of Bermuda* lands you.

The "Coralita" is one of the little ferries carrying people, bicycles across harbor.

16

Mid Ocean Club, located in Tucker's Town, was scene of meeting between President Eisenhower, Prime Minister Churchill, Premier Laniel and their aides.

"Old Maid's Lane" is typical of the old world charm found in the historic town of St. George. Visitors enjoy strolling or bicycling along the colorful streets.

Photos: Bermuda News Bureau

Jai Alai, one of the world's fastest games, is the most popular sport in Havana.

Morro Castle, fort at the entrance to Havana harbor, was built in the late 16th century as a protection against

Float of the Queen of Carnival takes place of honor in festival held each year.

CUBA HAS GAY DAYS AND NIGHTS

Cuba is by all odds the most popular island for U.S. visitors and its fascinating capital, Havana, is the place that most of them go. It's just a short hop from Miami by plane or boat, and you can go direct from New York or Chicago. Practically every cruise ship anchors in the harbor overnight. You can shop for perfume, alligator bags, cigars; there's the National Casino, Oriental Park, some of world's most exotic night life outside of Paris.

Photos: Morro Castle by A. L. Koolish; others by Cuban Tourist Commission

buccaneers. There's another Morro Castle at Santiago de Cuba, and still another at San Juan, Puerto Rico.

Torrid rhumbas are a feature of night clubs which offer most exotic night life.

The National Casino is the "Monte Carlo of America" with all games of chance.

Photos: Cuban Tourist Commission

19

San Francisco dock, in Havana harbor, is where the tender lands you from your ship anchored in the roadstead. It's just a short walk to Sloppy Joe's, Two Brothers.

The National Capitol dominates center of the metropolis, founded by Velasquez.

Nacional de Cuba is most famous hotel in the capital. New pool offers lush living.

Photos: A. L. Koolish; bottom left, Cuban Tourist Commission; right, Kirkeby Hotels

San Cristobal, known as the Columbus Cathedral, is over two hundred years old.

The Arts Building, recently opened, is representative of the present-day Havana.

Paseo de Marti (formerly "The Prado") runs from the center of Havana to the sea wall. Treelined, it reminds you of the Champs-Elysées, with its sidewalk cafés.

Photos: A. Milton Runyon; top right, Cuban Tourist Commission; bottom, Pan American World Airways

Christopher Columbus is, very naturally, a hero throughout the Caribbean. This monument to him is in the impressive courtyard of Municipal Palace, Havana.

Old Paula Church, now a National Monument, shows the older architecture.

Centro Asturiano Club has membership of 70,000. Building features marble stairs.

Photos: Charles Perry Weimer; bottom, Cuban Tourist Commission

Old and new combine: Havana's cobbled streets often open into broad boulevards.

Varadero Beach, Cuba's outstanding resort is easily reached by plane, car or bus.

La Concha Beach, right on the outskirts of Havana, in Marianao, is city's most popular for bathing. It has a pavilion, and facilities for boating, beach attractions.

Cuba is a world center for cigar-making. Here is interior of one of many factories.

Varadero Internacional Hotel is largest at the beach called "Rhapsody in Blue."

Photos: Cuban Tourist Commission; top right and center, Pan American World Airways

NASSAU IS PART OF THE ENCHANTING BAHAMAS

THE BRITISH COLONIAL HOTEL OFFERS TWO BEACHES, WATER-SKIING.

Nassau is less than an hour away from Miami by Pan American or BOAC, and the latter offers a 4½-hour direct flight from New York. You'll find it probably the most dignified of the British islands, peaceful, bucolic. The beaches are magnificent, and the climate almost always warm and sunny. The Bahamas are one of the world's great sportfishing grounds, abounding in tuna, sailfish, barracuda, bonito, wahoo, dolphin. And the Bay Street shops offer treasures from abroad.

Photo: A. Milton Runyon

At the Straw Market, in Rawson Square, you can buy straw hats, bags, table mats which are woven right before your eyes, and decorated with gaily colored shells.

Christ Church was designated as the Cathedral by Queen Victoria in 1861.

The British Colonial is Nassau's second largest hotel, with two beaches, pool.

Nassau

Paradise Beach is as famous as Waikiki. Surf temperature averages 70°, even in winter. Palm trees and sun-shelters add to its charm. Note cruise ships at anchor.

Prince George Dock is the place you get boat for short trip to Paradise Beach.

Horse and carriage await visitors at Royal Victoria Hotel's tropical gardens.

Photos: Nassau Development Board — Frederic Maura

Royal Victoria Hotel's new garden pool is surrounded by luxuriant trees, plants.

Bay Street is famed for shops offering British textiles, gloves, leather goods.

Queen's Staircase is 65-step man-made canyon, carved out of the solid coral rock.

Salt-water angling in Nassau is action-packed, for big game fisherman, amateur.

This octagonal building was once a jail; in 1879 it was converted into a library.

Fort Montagu Beach Hotel, seen from Fort Montagu, is Nassau's third largest.

Bahamas

Eleuthera is a large Bahama island east of New Providence which contains Nassau.

Governor's Harbor has miles of beaches and town with name of French Leave.

Walker Cay is one of 700 Bahama islets. Columbus made his first landfall on one.

Bimini is the Bahama island closest to the U.S., noted for its big game fishing.

28

SUMMER NEVER LEAVES JAMAICA

Largest British island in the West Indies, Jamaica offers beautiful mountain scenery, lovely beaches and good year 'round climate. Daytime temperatures are in the upper 70's all year, and trade winds make for cool nights.

Jamaica has five different resort areas: The first is the capital city of Kingston and suburban St. Andrews. At the eastern tip is Port Antonio and the northeast coast. Central Jamaica has Ocho Rios. Further west is Mandeville, its mountains and the south coast. And on the northwest coast is the famous Montego Bay.

Jamaica is 2½ hours from Miami by air, 6 hours from New York, and Kingston harbor is a port of call for many cruise ships. Part of the Greater Antilles, Jamaica is 140 miles long, 50 miles at its greatest width. It is 90 miles south of Cuba. Some of its mountains are as high as 7,000 feet.

Jamaican woman plaits hat from young leaves of the light jipijapa palm.

Noel Coward, English author and playwright, makes his island home at "Blue Harbour."

29

Jamaica

With razor sharp machete, this cutter is about to start on a field of sugar cane.

King Street is the shopping center of Kingston; place to buy English goods.

Flame blowers provide entertainment at night for visitors at Hotel Casa Blanca.

WATER SKIIERS SKIM PAST TOWER ISLE, JAMAICA'S $2,000,000 RESORT.

Photos: Jamaica Tourist Trade Development Board; center right, Gerald Murison, bottom, Pierre Chong

Fort Charles, 1656, and Palisadoes airport are on long peninsula that encloses harbor.

The south coast has many lakes where fishing is fun, and even washing clothes!

Doctor's Cave beach at Montego Bay is one of the finest in the entire Caribbean. It has fine white coral sand and sea water so clear that a boat floating on its surface seems to be floating in mid-air! Bathing is a constant delight, with no rough surf.

From near Berrydale, on the northeast coast, a 2½ mile sinuously curving stretch of gentle rapids on the Rio Grande is the route of the unique sport of river-rafting."

Montego Bay, with fashionable Sunset Lodge and Casa Blanca Hotel, is today the Cannes of Jamaica, even though only 35 years ago it was just a fishing village.

Photos: Vilma F. Bergane; bottom, Jamaica Tourist Trade Development Board

HAITI IS A "MAGIC ISLAND"

To appreciate Haiti, you'll want to know something of its strange history, of Toussaint L'Ouverture, of Dessalines, of Henri Christophe, Haiti's Black Napoleon who built the fabulous *Citadelle.* Read John Vandercook's *Black Majesty,* or William Seabrook's *The Magic Island,* or Kenneth Roberts' novel of Haiti, *Lydia Bailey.*

Haiti is one of the two Negro republics in the world, the other being Liberia. The official language is French, but most people speak a French patois called Creole.

Haiti is 4 hours by air from Miami. Panama Line ships call there.

Ubiquitous small boys, usually less well dressed, pose for your photos.

At Centre d'Art, see work of Louverture Poisson, other Haitian painters.

The Citadelle was built by Henri Christophe to stop French invasion that never came.

Photos: Pan American World Airways; top left, Jerry Hardy

La Basilique de Notre Dame, the Cathedral in Port-au-Prince, suggests Moorish influence in its design. Catholicism is predominant, but folk creeds are followed.

Sugar cane travels by ox-cart to narrow gauge railroad, then to mills for pressing.

Cutting the cane is hard work, too. Nowhere else do men live closer to the earth.

Photos: Pan American World Airways; bottom, Jerry Hardy

Port-au-Prince, called "the city of ten million roosters," is like no other capital. You'll see hundreds of women carrying baskets of produce on their heads.

Sugar, sisal, bananas and coffee are Haiti's chief products. The men farmers stay in the hills, working on their farms, while women carry produce to market.

Photos: Pan American World Airways; bottom, Tommy Hardy

TRUJILLO PEACE MONUMENT IS AT SANTIAGO DE LOS CABALLEROS.

THE DOMINICAN REPUBLIC COMBINES OLD AND NEW

Founded 1496 by Bartholomew Columbus, Ciudad Trujillo (formerly Santo Domingo) is the oldest permanent European settlement in the New World. Dominican Republic occupies eastern part of Hispaniola Island, Haiti western.

Photo: Dominican Republic Information Center

Christopher Columbus is most important in history of this land because it was on Hispaniola (Dominican Republic and Haiti) that he made his first real landing.

The Renaissance Cathedral in Ciudad Trujillo contains elaborate Columbus tomb.

The supposed bones of the explorer were transported here from Havana in 1898.

Dominican Republic

Almost leveled by a hurricane in 1930, Ciudad Trujillo has been rebuilt along clean, modern lines, making it one of the most attractive of Caribbean cities.

Hotel Jaragua, palatial, government-owned, is run by U.S. hotel operators, has swimming pool, tennis courts, golf course, surf breaking at the edge of its lawns.

Photos: Dominican Information Center; Copyright, Charles Perry Weimer

"SWITZERLAND OF THE AMERICAS" – PUERTO RICO

Part of the United States, yet distinctly foreign in its atmosphere, 100-mile-long Puerto Rico offers mountain scenery to rival the French and Swiss Alps, beautiful beaches, and a pleasant climate. The winter temperature averages 74.5° and the summer 80°, a difference of only 5.5°. San Juan is only 5½ to 6 hours by air from New York by Pan American or Eastern. Delta-C&S flies daily from New Orleans via Cuba, Haiti and Dominican Republic.

Condado Beach Hotel and Fabulous New Caribe Hilton Are Right on the Ocean.

Photo: Hamilton Wright

Puerto Rico

Porta Coeli, "gate of heaven," one of the oldest churches in the western hemisphere.

Flower market offers a profusion of exotic blooms from tropical gardens.

Luquillo Beach is a mile-long crescent, fringed with palms, near El Yunque forest.

University of Puerto Rico has many students and professors from U.S.A.

Photos: Hamilton Wright

El Morro, built in 1539 with ship ballast, guards entrance to San Juan harbor.

Caribe Hilton's distinctive feature is that its 300 rooms have private balconies.

Condado Beach Hotel has been newly renovated, and a new mountain resort, El Barranquitas, has just opened. Best known country club is the Berwind, Rio Piedras.

Native net fisherman demonstrates possibilities for the sportsman. Puerto Rican waters are fished for white and blue marlin, sailfish, Allison tuna, many others.

Puerto Rico

Fiesta Santiago, celebrated for over 300 years by the villagers of Loíza Aldea, produces weird faces in coconut masks. Pageantry and parades last two weeks.

Shops in San Juan feature mahogany bowls, boxes, beautiful needlework. "Sunlight" factories offer blouses of lawn and linen with exquisitely delicate embroidery.

Photos: Hamilton Wright

Napoleon's Empress Josephine was born in Trois-Ilets, and a marble statue of her rises in the center of the Savannah or public park in city of Fort-de-France.

MARTINIQUE IS "POMPEII OF THE WEST INDIES"

On May 8, 1902 Mont Pelée blew up with a roar and wiped out the whole 40,000 population of St. Pierre, with just one survivor, a prisoner in an underground dungeon. Martinique is one of the two main French islands in the lesser Antilles, the other being Guadeloupe. 50 miles long by 19 wide, Martinique is very beautiful and a good place for relaxing because there's no night life. By plane it's 4½ hours from San Juan, Puerto Rico; by ship from New York, 8 days.

Native net-thrower fishermen in Ville-Fontaine show tourists how net is made.

Important influence of Roman Catholic Church has helped control communists.

Colorful costumes indicate native gaiety, also shown in dancing at *Select Tango*.

Lido Hotel, four miles from Fort-de-France, is place for bathing and loafing.

Vieux Moulin, Chez Etienne, L'Auberge de Manoir offer good French cuisine.

Photos: Pan American World Airways

GUADELOUPE KEEPS ALIVE ITS CREOLE HERITAGE

About 80 miles north of Martinique, the other French possession of Guadeloupe is one of those "get-away-from-it-all" places where accommodations are far from luxurious, but the climate is ideal, scenery superb, and natives interesting.

Pointe-à-Pitre is the principal city and port. The official capital is Basse-Terre, about forty miles away. A jeepable track leads to the base of the extinct volcano, La Soufrière, a good stiff climb. People keep alive gay Creole customs.

DISCOVER ANTIGUA FOR FRIENDLINESS

The coral island of Antigua is a British crown colony, capital of the Leeward Islands. It is a quiet, friendly place where every visitor is treated as an honored guest. St. John's is only 3 hours' flying time from San Juan, Puerto Rico.

Guests at the Mill Reef Club enjoy a sunlit terrace overlooking the white sand beaches and clear blue-green water. Antigua has swimming, tennis and golf.

Old winches like this were used to haul Lord Nelson's ships onto beach for repair.

Fishing boats may be chartered; waters near reefs are perfect for spear-fishing.

Photos: Pan American World Airways

EX-DANISH VIRGIN ISLANDS
ARE TRANQUIL, CHARMING

HILLSIDE STREETS OF CHARLOTTE AMALIE HAVE FLOWERING VINES.

Purchased from Denmark in 1917, for $25,000,000, the three main American Virgin Islands of St. Thomas, St. Croix and St. John are still unspoiled by too many tourists. Since they have free-port status, it is possible to buy many wonderful things at a fraction of their U.S. prices. Most visitors come for the wonderful climate, with an average mean temperature of 79° F., the bucolic atmosphere, the delight of being "abroad" and yet still on home territory.

St. Thomas is 80 miles east of Puerto Rico, 25 minutes by air. The entire plane trip from New York, via Eastern or Pan American takes about 6½ hours. Cruise ships frequently call at Charlotte Amalie, the port of St. Thomas.

St. Thomas is most highly developed island, with the new Virgin Isle and many fine hotels. St. Croix is the largest, most agricultural, with small but good hotels. St. John has most rugged primitiveness, limited but very delightful guest houses.

Virgin Islands

Distinctive tower features Bluebeard's Castle Hotel, setting for many legends.

Virgin Isle Hotel is newest, luxurious. Swimming pool overlooks hills, harbor.

From the terrace of Bluebeard's Castle Hotel, you look out over the whole town

Photos: Pan American World Airways; top left, A. Milton Runyon; bottom left, Virgin Isle Hotel

of Charlotte Amalie. On far side is the French village, called Cha-Cha Town, whose people are descendants of the early French settlers. Shrine of St. Anne is here.

Virgin Islands

Cruise ship "Mauretania" stays in harbor, ferries passengers to dock by motorboat.

Steep streets of Charlotte Amalie often require steps from one level to another.

Three youngsters grin for the tourist-photographer in hope of U.S. pennies.

Magen's Bay beach is on Atlantic side of St. Thomas; Morning Star on Caribbean.

Christiansted on northeast (above) and Frederiksted on the west are the two principal towns on St. Croix.

This old Danish sugar mill is St. Croix Island landmark.

Photos: A. Milton Runyon; bottom row, Pan American World Airways

TRINIDAD IS THE CAPITAL OF CALYPSO

ON DRIVE "OVER THE SADDLE" TO MARACAS BAY YOU PAUSE HERE.

Most colorful and polyglot of all the West Indies islands, Trinidad is home of Calypso, the satirical and haunting folk songs. As you walk through the streets of the capital, Port of Spain, you're likely to encounter East Indians, Hindus, British, Spanish, French, Chinese, Africans, Americans. There are Moslem mosques, Hindu temples, bazaars. Port of Spain is 9 hours' flying time from New York.

51

Beautiful Maracas Bay, on North Coast, is reached by drive from Port of Spain that winds through bamboo groves, banyan trees, coffee and cocoa plantations.

Donkey cart loaded with coconuts is the Trinidad version of sidewalk "milk bar."

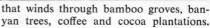

Frederick Street is Port of Spain's shopping center for British goods, silver.

52

Pitch Lake (Asphalt) is supposed to be 285 feet deep. You can walk on surface.

A Sikh, one of many East Indians living in Trinidad, stands before a mosque.

The local "steel bands" consist of steel drums of varying tones beaten to Calypso rhythm. The effect is surprisingly good. January is month of Calypso competition.

Queen's Park Hotel, center of social life, is located on 200-acre Savannah.

Trinidad's fertile soil yields sugar cane, cacao, coffee, citrus fruits, coconuts.

Photos: Trinidad and
Tobago Tourist Board

TOBAGO IS UNSPOILED

Believed to be the spot where Robinson Crusoe was shipwrecked, Tobago is little-known place whose visitors would like to preserve its charm for themselves alone.

Aquatic Club beach has cabanas thatched with palm leaves and wonderful beach. It's at Pigeon Point, Man of War Bay. With sea goggles you may look at marine life.

Exotic birds of paradise are found only in Tobago and in New Guinea. They're shy, hard to find, but it's an unforgettable experience to see them on this tiny isle.

Tobago is a land of leisure and quiet beauty that you have often longed for. There are four main hotels and one guest house, an indication of the privacy here.

54

WILLEMSTAD, BISECTED BY ST. ANNA BAY, HAS PONTOON BRIDGE.

OIL BRINGS RICHES
TO DUTCH INDIES

The Netherlands West Indies consist of two widely separated units: the islands of Curaçao, Aruba and Bonaire, off the coast of Venezuela, and 500 miles away in the Lesser Antilles, the islands of Saba, St. Eustatius and southern half of St. Martin (the other half being French). A one-stop flight from New York brings you to Curaçao in less than 10 hours.

Photo: Netherlands West Indies Tourist Committee

Bird's-eye view of Willemstad shows two halves, joined by "Queen Emma" bridge.

CURAÇAO MIGHT BE HOLLAND AT SEA

Peter Stuyvesant became governor of Curaçao in 1643 and moved to New Amsterdam, now New York, in 1647. For 17 years he was Director General of the New Netherlands and Netherlands West Indies. Formerly a colony, this territory became in 1922 an integral part of the kingdom of the Netherlands. At first glance it looks like a slice of Holland, tidy and well scrubbed, moved out into the Atlantic 40 miles north of Venezuela. But you soon notice the West Indies influence. The buildings come in pastel, and sometimes more violent tints to soften the glare.

Passengers on cruise steamer get view of pontoon bridge as it swings to side.

Piscadera Bay Club, foremost resort, has natural swimming pool with sea water.

Everything but liquor and tobacco is imported at 3.3% duty; it's almost free port.

Floating market forms daily on older side of town, with schooners from many ports.

Foodstuffs are peddled right from the decks. Many merchants are Venezuelan.

West Point Bay and beach, at the western tip of Curaçao, is a popular drive from Willemstad for lunch, bathing and fishing. Aloes cactus flourishes here.

Photos: Netherlands West Indies Tourist Committee

Netherlands West Indies

Aruba is most important oil refining center. Its Fort Zoutman is relic of past.

Palm Beach, on Aruba, one of finest, is three miles of white sand, clear water.

As on most Caribbean islands, fishing is important for food as well as sport.

Nassaustraat, Oranjestad, offers modern shops, old bazaars selling varied goods.

Bonaire, 30 miles east of Curaçao, has changed little in the past century. Noted as a paradise for birds, its salt-water bays are sanctuaries for odd flamingoes

Photos: Netherlands West Indies Tourist Committee

The three Netherlands Windward Islands
lie 550 miles northeast of Curaçao.

Saba's capital is called "The Bottom."
The others are St. Martin, St. Eustatius.

An old man of Bonaire
repairs his fish net.

The transportation of water is
frequently by donkey-drawn cart.

The women spend time
in making needlework.

Photos: Netherlands West Indies Tourist
Committee; bottom center, Richard Joseph.

BARBADOS IS A TROPICAL BRITAIN

Said to have been originally discovered by the Portuguese and named "Los Barbados" because of the bearded fig trees, Barbados was claimed by the British in 1605, settled by them beginning in 1627, and has been under the British flag ever since—something quite unusual in the history of a Caribbean island. Most easterly of the West Indies, Barbados is 1¼ hours by airplane from Port of Spain.

Sam Lord's Castle, at St. Philip, is now operated as a residential club, one of several on Barbados, and there are good small hotels. Life is simple, leisurely

Photos: Barbado
Publicity Committe

Excellent roads criss-cross Barbados Island, with its very English landscape.

Swan Street, Bridgetown, is filled with carts, cyclists, autos, and pedestrians.

The Savannah, big oblong of grass, is used for polo matches, race meetings.

At races the police band plays; the little horses bear colors raced for generations.

Photos: Barbados
Publicity Committee

GRENADA IS "THE SPICE ISLAND"

Most southerly of the Windward Islands, Grenada is famous for its nutmeg, clove, and for some of the most beautiful white sand beaches in the world. It has Grand Étang, spectacular volcanic lake 1740 ft. above sea level. Grenada is just 50 minutes' flying time from Port of Spain.

Morne Rouge Beach Club, St. George's, has excellent beach, dining and dancing.

Another fine spot to swim, or dream, is Grand Anse, with two miles of white sand.

Guests of the Santa Maria Hotel enjoy tea on veranda overlooking picturesque

St. George's. Its red-roofed houses ar pale pink and green, its atmosphere quie

Carenage Bay is a calm harbor for fishing boats and cargo schooners. One section of St. George's is on the bay, another on the sea, connected by tunnel.

Photo: Pan American World Airways

63

ST. LUCIA WAS PORT FOR CLIPPER SHIPS

Directly in the path of the trade winds on route of the sailing clippers of old, St. Lucia is largest of Windward Islands. Castries has sheltered harbor, one of finest in the West Indies and long an important coaling station. Landmarks are mineral springs near Soufrière and cones of the Twin Pitons Peaks. Castries is just 2 hours by air from Port of Spain.

Hotel Antoine is high on a hill overlooking the city of Castries, its harbor and background of chocolate drop hills Pigeon Island Beach Club is charming

Photo: Pan American World Airways

Voyage 2
CANADA AND ALASKA

S.S. "EMPRESS OF SCOTLAND" SAILS FROM LIVERPOOL TO QUEBEC.

Because many parts of the United States are hot in the summer, nearby Canada has become a favorite vacation ground, offering cool lakes, rivers, beautiful mountains. And in winter, snow for sports is abundant in the Laurentians and Canadian Rockies.

One of Canada's many advantages is its excellent transportation. Canadian Pacific and Canadian National cover it with great railroad networks. There are Great Lakes steamers and St. Lawrence River steamers. Trans-Canada Air Lines will take you across Canada, or abroad. And because the highways are excellent, and less likely to be crowded, many tourists prefer to travel by car, especially on such a scenic drive as the one around the Gaspé Peninsula between Maine and the St. Lawrence. Another excellent idea is to make

your trip abroad by way of the St. Lawrence River. You embark either at Montreal or Quebec on a white Canadian Pacific liner and travel nearly a thousand miles in the quiet river waters before you get to the open ocean, and you can get a very good idea of Canada on the way. On the west coast, Canada is the gateway to Alaska, via the 1000-mile "inside passage" route from Victoria and Vancouver up Georgia Strait, Queen Charlotte Strait to Prince Rupert, Juneau and Skagway.

In visiting Canada you will meet the warm friendship of good neighbors. You cross the border without fuss, you need no passport, suffer no restrictions. You'll be amazed at the industrial developments in many places, but you'll enjoy some of the world's great resorts and national parks covering 29,000 square miles.

Photo: Canadian
Pacific Railway

CHATEAU FRONTENAC HOTEL IS LIKE A MEDIEVAL FRENCH CASTLE.

QUEBEC HAS CHARM
OF THE OLD WORLD

Discovered by Jacques Cartier in 1534 and settled by the French under Champlain early in the 17th century, Quebec hasn't lost its Old World flavor. Hand looms, outdoor bake ovens, spinning wheels are still in daily use. Although French is spoken throughout the province, most people also speak English.

Photo: Canadian
Pacific Railway

Calèches haul tourists up and down the hills as the driver tells of historic spots.

Rue Sous-le-Cap, in Lower Town, is said to be narrowest street in North America.

Quebec is deeply religious city, with Sisters of the Good Shepherd, and many shrines.

St. Louis Gate is one of several remaining from old fortifications of early days

Hooked rugs, made during long winters, are good buys; so are carved wood figures.

Curling is kind of bowling played with heavy stones slid along ice toward a mark

Photos: Canadian Pacific Railway
top left, Canadian National Railway

Chateau Frontenac's toboggan slide takes you at mile-a-minute speed from near top of Citadel hill down to Dufferin Terrace with spectacular view of St. Lawrence.

Photo: Canadian
Pacific Railway

Ste. Anne de Beaupré, a few miles east of Quebec City, is most famous shrine of the New World. The great Basilica burned in 1922, but has been built anew.

Scala Sancta, sacred stairway at Ste. Anne, is worn by the knees of worshipers.

Montmorency Falls, between Quebec and Ste. Anne, are even higher than Niagara

Photos: Canadian Government Trave Bureau; top, Canadian Pacific Railway

Round Lake Inn, Weir, is one of many resorts of Quebec and the Laurentians.

Laurentides Park and Mt. Tremblant Park have 1500 lakes and cascading streams.

Maple sugar camps in the Laurentians gather their annual harvest each spring.

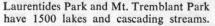

Many a rural Quebec family still goes to Mass on Sunday in a horse-drawn buggy.

Husky races are one of Canada's many winter sports: Scandinavian-type skiing in the east, the dashing Alpine kind in western Rockies; skating, hockey, curling.

Bonaventure Island, off end of Gaspé peninsula, is a sanctuary for gannets.

River steamer of Canada Steamship Lines passes Manoir Richelieu, at Murray Bay.

Old Habitant houses like this one on Isle of Orleans have been lived in 200 years.

Percé Rock is the high point of tour around Gaspé peninsula. It's the pierced rock that Cartier first saw beside the shore, a great stone buffeted by seas

Photos: Canada Steamship Lines; Canadian National Railways; Canadian Pacific Railway; Office Provincial de Publicité, Quebec

Mount Royal, towering above the great city of Montreal, second largest French-speaking city in the world, has a lookout that gives magnificent view of the city.

Open sightseeing trolley cars are unique way to take in Montreal's historic points.

Bonsecours Market is the place where the habitant farmers sell their own produce.

Photos: Canadian National Railways; bottom right, Canadian Pacific Railway

73

Brother André's first chapel in Montreal.

St. Joseph's Oratory draws stream of pilgrims every day.

St. Catherine Street is one of the main shopping centers.

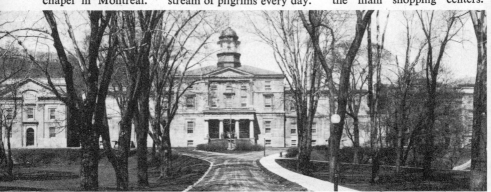

The fame of McGill University has gone around the world, especially for its medicine. Some think ice hockey was invented at McGill. Now skiing has taken over.

Montreal is the world's largest grain-shipping port, transshipment point for Great Lakes. Its extensive docks are busy when St. Lawrence is not ice-blocked.

Canada NOVA SCOTIA

Grand Pré was home of Longfellow's *Evangeline*.

Evangeline's Memorial is in a park full of flowers, memories.

Chester Inlet is quiet spot on the south shore.

Port Royal Habitation was first permanent white settlement north of the Gulf.

From Dingwall, Cape Breton Island, boats fish most fertile waters for swordfish, tuna.

Old shipmodeler at Plympton works on craft that brings back exciting memories.

Ox cart plods through village of Shag Harbour, known for its lobster, fisheries.

Photos: Canadian Pacific Railway; top right, Canadian National Railways; center right, Canadian Government Travel Bureau

St. Andrews-by-the-Sea is world-famous resort.

Antique-hunting, fishing, golf, are attractions at St. Andrews.

Country around Greenock Church looks Scottish.

Famous "Reversing Falls" at St. John are due to tremendous tides in Bay of Fundy.

As tide rises, the falls run uphill, inland from the sea, then they reverse.

Fundy National Park rises above tide-worn cliffs. It has sea and fresh-water swimming and fishing, including the heated salt-water swimming pool pictured

Photos: Canadian Pacific Railway; bottom, Canadian Government Travel Bureau

Nine to thirty miles off Canada's coast, Prince Edward Island is reached by ferry.

Articles of Confederation, making Canada a Dominion, were drawn at Charlottetown.

The crack clipper ship, *Marco Polo,* was wrecked off Cavendish. The beach, now part of the Prince Edward Island National Park, is best-known resort on the Island.

Photos: Canadian National Railways; bottom, Canadian Government Travel Bureau

Canada NEWFOUNDLAND

Gander Airport is main North American terminal for air services to all parts of Europe, built 1939. Though there is heavy snow, Gander is relatively free from fog.

Lumbering is important Newfoundland industry; there are plants for woodworking.

At Cabot Tower, St. John's, Marconi received first wireless across the Atlantic.

Fishing (cod, salmon, herring, lobster) on the Grand Banks and Labrador coast is the chief occupation. Newfoundland joined Confederation on March 31, 1949.

78

Photos: Canadian National Railways top, Canadian Government Travel Bureau

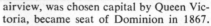

Ottawa, whose Parliament buildings on bank of Ottawa River are shown in this airview, was chosen capital by Queen Victoria, became seat of Dominion in 1867.

Fort Henry, overlooking Kingston harbor, built in 1812, is now history museum.

Ship passes through the Long Soo Canal. In background you see Long Soo Rapids.

Peace Tower is the dominating feature of Parliament buildings, rebuilt after fire.

Photos: Canadian Pacific Railway; center and bottom left, Canadian Government Travel Bureau

This is one of lakes in the Haliburton district, near Algonquin Provincial Park.

Best vantage point for the widest-angle view of Niagara Falls in the attractive

Toronto, on Lake Ontario, is Canada's second city, business center of flourishing

Ontario industry. Since 1912, Canadian National Exposition has been held here.

Photos: Herbert Ford; top right, Canadian Pacific Railway; bottom, Canadian Government Travel Bureau

top-floor big-windowed dining room of the General Brock Hotel. You can watch the *Maid-of-the-Mist* take honeymooners for an exciting close-up near the falls.

Queen Elizabeth Way is excellent highway running from Niagara Falls to Toronto.

Steamer "Sagamo" plies Muskoka Lakes, forest-resort region north of Toronto.

Photos: Canadian Government Travel Bureau; bottom right, Herbert Ford

This angler's paradise is near border, west Ontario; others are more remote.

Fishermen at this lodge go after large and smallmouth bass, northern pike, and trout.

Fish grow big in Ontario's 750,000 lakes and ponds, and its many lively streams.

Fishermen's village is near Kenora, Lake of the Woods, 120 miles east of Winnipeg.

Sampling the fresh-caught trout sizzling over campfire is one of real delights

Photos: A. L. Koolis

Winnipeg, capital of Manitoba, is midway between Atlantic and Pacific. It is distributing center for Prairie Provinces and largest wheat market, grain exchange.

World's largest privately owned railway yards are Canadian Pacific's at Winnipeg.

A self-propelled combine harvests barley in the vicinity of St. François Xavier.

Riding Mountain National Park, 100 miles north of Winnipeg, has hotels, cabins.

At Churchill, on Hudson Bay, grain is loaded for trip through Hudson Strait.

Photos: Canadian National Railways; center, Canadian Pacific Railway; bottom left, Canadian Government Travel Bureau

Canada SASKATCHEWAN, ALBERTA

Regina, capital of Saskatchewan, is the first training center for famous Royal Canadian Mounted Police recruits. Above is Hotel Saskatchewan. City has many parks.

Prince Albert National Park and eight provincial parks in Saskatchewan provide many miles of forests, lakes, rivers. This is air view of Waskesiu and Lake Waskesiu.

The magnificent Banff Springs Hotel has a most spectacular setting overlooking the Bow River Valley. It's right in the Rockies, at an altitude of 4,538 feet.

84

and is surrounded by several peaks over 9,000 feet high. Banff is in southern part of Banff National Park, 65 miles west of Calgary, and is famous as both summer and winter resort, with hot sulphur springs, museum, zoological garden, wild-animal paddock. For 64 years the Indian Days celebrations have been held here.

The Canadian Rockies are North American center of Alpine skiing, with snow 20 feet deep and powder fast. The peaks of the Rockies provide a majestic backdrop.

Behind the Banff ski lift you see peak of Mount Rundle, with Bow River Valley.

Along the Banff-Lake Louise highway you stop to feed Rocky Mountain sheep

Photos: Canadian Pacific Railway; bottom right, Canadian Government Travel Bureau

Banff Indian Days, with their contests, reach climax with awards at the Hotel.

Chieftains parade in all their finery: Crees, Saracees, Blackfeet, and Stonys.

Banff School of Fine Arts, an extension of the University of Alberta, has held summer courses at Banff for twenty years. Students have beautiful scenes to paint.

Canada ALBERTA

Lake Louise, near Banff—sapphire blue in color and surrounded by perpetually snow-capped peaks—has been called mos' beautiful single scene in North America

Six Glaciers Tea House looks out on Lake Louise and 11,365-foot Mount Victoria.

Trail Riders' packtrain crosses shallo' Pipestone River on way to base cam

Photos: Canadie
Pacific Railw

Canoeing is probably best way to enjoy full beauty of Lake Louise and the giddy summits around it, in their ever-changing panorama. You may see bighorn sheep.

Photo: Canadian Pacific Railway.

Chuck-wagon racers thunder into last lap of half-mile gallop at Calgary Stampede.

Jasper Park Lodge, built of fieldstone, logs, fits its surroundings beautifully.

Over 300,000 spectators attend Calgary Stampede to watch racing, riding, roping.

Dining Room of new central building at the Lodge has great picture-window views.

Storm clouds hover over Mount Assiniboine as file of Trail Riders nears camp.

For nearly thirty years the Trail Riders have made their annual Rockies camp trip.

At Mount Warren, Jasper Park, sportsmen discover excitement of mountain climbing.

Immense crevasse-riven glacier of the Columbia Icefield is awe-inspiring sight.

Castle Mountain, between Lake Louise and Banff, is now Mount Eisenhower.

Scarlet-coated Royal Canadian "mounties" are on duty in all the national parks.

Steamer "Princess Elizabeth" pulls into pier at Nanaimo, Vancouver Island. Such steamers ply daily between Victoria, Vancouver and Inside Passage to Alaska.

Founded in 1843 by Hudson's Bay Company as a fur trading post, Victoria is now capital of British Columbia. Empress Hotel is attractive; roses bloom all year.

Lumber, pulp are important. Logs are dumped at Chemainus, Vancouver Island.

Thunderbird Park is one of several i Victoria; others are Beacon Hill, Gorg

Photos: Canadian Government Travel Bureo center and left, Canadian Pacific Railwo bottom right, Canadian National Railwo

Vancouver is one of the most beautiful cities in Canada. Here its impressive skyline and busy port is seen from Royal Vancouver Rowing Club across the harbor.

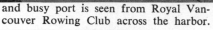

Emperor Falls, near Mt. Robson, is typical of majestic scenery in British Columbia.

Two notable features of Vancouver are Lions Gate Bridge (above), Stanley Park.

Photos: Canadian Government Travel Bureau; Canadian Pacific Railway; Canadian National Railways

ALASKA IS LAST FRONTIER OF U.S.

Alaska is easily reached by plane, or by Inside Passage as far north as Juneau, and from there across the Gulf of Alaska to Prince William Sound. This beautiful trip visits the main industrial cities. Within Alaska, planes are used for long distance runs, dog teams for short ones. The Alaska Railroad serves the gold mines, coal fields, Mt. McKinley National Park.

ALASKA'S FIRST GOLD RUSH RESULTED IN FOUNDING OF JUNEAU

Mendenhall Glacier is one of the few that can be reached by automobile road.

Salmon fishing areas are not far from Juneau; fresh water fish are abundant

94

Fairbanks is center for tourists who arrive by Yukon River from Whitehorse.

Eskimo family at Nome keeps busy making shoes from walrus hide, carving ivory.

Started as a supply point for miners in 90's rush, Ketchikan is usually first Alaska community visited by tourists. Hundreds of fishing vessels use good port.

Photos: Pan American World Airways

Indian Meeting House and totem poles are
seen at Totem Village, near Ketchikan.

Cruise steamer, bound north, passe
through Lynn Canal in sight of glaciers

Mt. McKinley National Park is second in
size only to Yellowstone. This wilderness

is topped by Mt. McKinley, 20,270 fee
the highest point in all North Americ

Gold dust and nuggets in the Miners and
Merchants Bank are melted into ingots.

This bus is on Alaska Highway, 1527 mil
long, Dawson Creek, B.C., to Fairbanl

96

Voyage 3
MEXICO AND CENTRAL AMERICA

Just as Canada is a handy "foreign" vacationland on the north, so are Mexico and Central America on the south—and especially so for the residents of the border states of California, Arizona, New Mexico, Texas and other states near enough for travel by car. The well-paved Inter-American Highway leads from Laredo, Texas, through Monterrey to Mexico City, a comfortable 3-day trip of 764 miles. If you're coming from the East, you could cross the border at Brownsville and join the main highway at Ciudad Victoria. From California and Arizona, a popular auto trip south is through the Mexican state of Sonora which has recently been hard-topping its roads and preparing for North American visitors. From Nogales, just south of Tucson, Arizona, you head for Hermosillo and Guaymas. On the Gulf of California is the fishing mecca of Puerto Peñasco.

Air travel takes you speedily to Mexico City and other Central American points. Pan American has a network of routes serving all the principal points. American Airlines uses Dallas as take-off point for Mexico City. Guest Airways, Braniff and others cover different points.

The United Fruit steamers call at Guatemala, Honduras and Panama Canal ports. Standard Fruit Line

Basket vendor waits beside a Taxco road.

and others offer service by passenger-carrying freighters. Panama Line sails from New York to canal ports. By railroad, you can go from New York to Mexico City in three days and three nights, from St. Louis in two days and two nights. And if you wish, you can go all the way on down to Guatemala City by rail.

Whichever way you come, you're sure to find real Latin hospitality in the "My house is yours" tradition.

OLD SPAIN LIVES IN MODERN MEXICO

THIS GATE OPENS ON VERSAILLES-LIKE CHAPULTEPEC CASTLE, PARK.

Travelers from the U.S. are spending more than 180 million dollars a year in Mexico, land of the ancient Aztecs, where the charm of Old Spain lives on in a magnificent modern setting. By air, Mexico City is 8 hours from Los Angeles, 3¼ hours from Brownsville, Texas. Or go by train, bus, ship, automobile.

The Zócalo, old Mexico City square, is setting for the great cathedral, Church of the Asunción de María Santísima. The foundation is on stones of Aztec temple

Dressed for the Fiesta: There are many festivals, some local, some nation-wide.

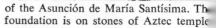

Benito Juárez, memorial above, was the leader who instituted the Reform Laws

Photos: Ewing Galloway; bottom left, A. L. Koorish; bottom right, Pan American World Airways

Palace of Fine Arts is center of art and music, with National Theater, murals.

The National Palace, with offices of the President, flanks east side of the Zócalo.

Hotel Reforma has 25 skyline suites looking out over the nearby mountains.

Paseo de la Reforma leads from center of Mexico City to Chapultepec Castle.

Modern business section is at crossing of Avenida Juárez, Paseo de la Reforma.

From fashionable symphony of Chávez to strolling players, Mexico is musical.

Temple of Quetzalcoatl, the wind god of the ancient Toltec civilization which preceded the Aztecs, is 29 miles from Mexico City, at San Juan Teotihuacán

The great Pyramid of the Sun is also at San Juan Teotihuacán. Once used as altar and observatory, it is 217 feet high has bigger base than Pyramid of Cheops

Photos: A. L. Koolish; bottom Burton Holmes (Ewing Galloway)

Plaza de Toros: Mexico City's bull ring is largest bullfighting arena in world.

Pre-fight ceremonies and parade have a fascinating array of color and costume.

Bullfight begins with grand entry of all the bull's antagonists: Three toreros, three banderilleros, three picadors, and the matador, who is responsible for the kill.

Action of bullfight is effectively told in Hemingway's *Death in the Afternoon*.

The audience at a bullfight is perhaps most interesting part of the spectacle.

Floating Gardens of Xochimilco are most popular on Sundays when people of all social classes come to ride the flower decked boats, poled by Aztec Indians

Xochimilco punts are called *canoas*, are furnished with chairs and table for food.

Chapultepec Park is one of world's most lovely natural parks, with shaded walks

104

Photos: Kurt Severin (Black Star); bottom left, Pan American World Airways; bottom right, Victor de Palma (Black Star

Festivals, like this Harvest festival at Ocoyoacac, are very colorful, interesting.

Conversation piece: From balcony of your hotel you observe scenes like this.

Inter-American Highway traffic at Zima-pán: This road is great building achieve-ment, sometimes at sea level, sometimes rising to heights more than 8,000 feet.

Massive cathedral in Cuernavaca was begun by Cortez in 1529, is very Spanish in character. Much of the city retain atmosphere of days of the conquistadore

Tepoztlán, Aztec for *Where there is Copper,* puts on an outstanding festival.

Teloztlán, unspoiled village 12 miles fro Cuernavaca, adheres to old ways of li

Photos: Georgia Engelhard (Cam Clix); bottom, Samuel E. Less

Community laundry is a feature of old picturesque silver-mining town of Taxco.

Perched on side of a mountain, Taxco rivals the hill towns of Italy for beauty.

"Heavy Traffic" in fascinating Taxco: there's "a picture around every corner."

Indian market, on Sundays, offers baskets, silver, tinware, many other handicrafts.

Photos: A. L. Koolish; top right,
Georgia Engelhard (Camera Clix)

Cathedral at Oaxaca is still lovely in spite of damage by quakes, revolutions.

Hall of Monoliths is most interesting room in the Mitla Ruins, near Oaxaca

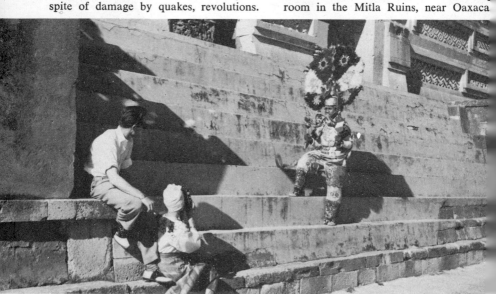

Feather dancer entertains visitors on steps of Palace, in the Mitla Ruins.

These great pre-Conquest buildings were constructed entirely without metal tools

Photos: Pan American World Airways
top right, Arthur Center (Black Star

Native market at summer resort of Toluca has artistic pottery, other handicrafts.

Guadalajara's beautiful city hall is feature of Mexico's 2nd largest city.

Lake Pátzcuaro, known as "the disappearing lake," is the highest navigable body of water in Mexico. It abounds in fish, which natives catch with "butterfly" nets.

Mexico

Morelia's main square: Towers of great cathedral are more than 200 feet high.

Aqueduct at Morelia was built, 1785–8 to give employment during a famir

Spectacular mountains and lush tropical foliage are reflected in swimming pool near Veracruz, city whose name sten from Cortez landing on Good Frida

Amecameca ("Many Water Holes" in Aztec) is point of ascent to Popocatepetl and Ixtaccihuatl (in background of photo), the two magnificent volcanoes.

El Castillo is huge 100-foot pyramid at Maya ruins of Chichén Itzá, near Mérida.

Temple of the Warriors surrounds 4½ acre area that was probably a Mayan market.

Church of San Francisco at San Miguel de Allende is in Spanish colonial style.

Monterrey, 3rd largest city, is 140 mi. from Laredo, on Inter-Am. Highway.

Photos: De Cou (Ewing Galloway); center left, A. L. Koolish; center right, Jim Mitchell (Black Star); bottom left, George Pickow (Three Lions); bottom right, Burton Holmes (Ewing Galloway)

Deep-sea fishing is famous at Acapulco; witness this magnificent sailfish catch.

Favorite "morning" beach is Caleta. In the afternoon, Los Hornos is preferred.

Photos: A. L. Koolish

El Mirador Hotel, on Quebrada Cliffs, (below) has a magnificent water view.

Daredevil divers leap from 100-foot cliff into waters between Quebrada rocks.

Photo: Above, Eric M. Sanford (Black Star)   **113**

Some of the world's most beautiful vistas
are to be seen from the Quebrada rocks
and other points near Acapulco. Town is
one of oldest ports on the Pacific coast

Photo: A L. Koolish

Reforma Casablanca Hotel stands high on a hill, with wonderful view. The hotel has a lovely patio and terraces, salt-water swimming pool, and two cabarets.

Fishermen's Wharf: You may hire launches here by the hour, to go after swordfish, sailfish, other tropical varieties. If you prefer hunting, hills have deer.

Photos: A. L. Koolish

Mexico

Loaves of bread aren't cellophane-wrapped in rural areas, but taste is good!

The festival for blessing the sugar cane: almost every day sees a fiesta somewhere.

Mexican musicians start young, and play impromptu concerts anywhere, any time.

This is the sort of café entertainment you get anywhere in the south of Mexico.

Street merchant in Oaxaca offers Aztec patterns in hand-loomed cotton and wool.

Mexicans excel in making costumes out of things at hand; note inverted lampshades

Photos: Samuel E. Lesser

GUATEMALA IS LAND OF HILLS AND LAKES

If you're seeking a land of great scenic beauty, with jungle highlands, ancient cathedrals, Indian villages, you'll find them all in Guatemala. But you won't get night life or conventional entertainment.

Calvary Church, built 1618, is located at Chichicastenango, the Indian village that is a "must" for Guatemalan visitors. Faithful worshipers come by thousands.

Photo: National Tour-
t Bureau, Guatemala

Guatemala

Lake Atitlán is 67 miles in circumference and is flanked by three volcanoes. Around the beautiful lake are a dozen villages which are named after the 12 apostles.

Pottery is made by Indian artisans who seldom use the same exotic design twice.

At market, you can identify Indians from different villages by distinctive dress.

Photos: National Tourist Bureau, Guatemala; bottom right, Richard Josep

"Conquest Dance"—one of most colorful Indian ceremonial dances—is performed at Chichicastenango. It represents fight between Indians and Spaniards in 1558.

Guatemala City was almost entirely destroyed by earthquake in 1917, has since been rebuilt along clean, modern lines. National Palace has interesting murals.

Photos: National Tourist Bureau, Guatemala; bottom, Pan American World Airways

COFFEE DOMINATES ECONOMIC
LIFE OF TINY EL SALVADOR

El Salvador is almost a one-crop nation, coffee—mostly of the "mild" variety—furnishing 80% of all exports. Country has 170 mile coastline on Pacific, but none on Atlantic, is not easily reached.

Smallest of the Central American republics, El Salvador is the most densely populated, with 144 persons per square mile. The climate is subtropical, with moderately heavy rainfall of 68 inches.

San Salvador, capital of El Salvador, centers on Parque Barrios, with the National Palace (above) being the most imposing building in city of 160,000

Photo: El Salvador Government

Tegucigalpa was founded 1578 as mining settlement, became capital of Honduras in 1880. City centers on Plaza Morazán, site of cathedral and municipal palace.

HONDURAS EXPORTS ITS BANANA GOLD

Bananas, the golden agricultural crop of Honduras, are grown in the north on plantations once run by big U.S. fruit companies, now controlled by local interests. It's little-known by tourists.

Inspector looks over bananas. At left, Mayan seat in the park at Tegucigalpa.

121

NICARAGUA OFFERS SECOND CANAL SITE

Lake Nicaragua, Lake Managua and the Tipitapa River that connects them have long been considered for a canal from the Atlantic to the Pacific. Nicaragua is largely mountainous, thinly peopled.

La Merced church is one of many colonial churches in León, once the capital.

Las Isletas, in Granada, is lovely area reached by the Inter-American highway.

Managua was made capital of Nicaragua in 1855 to end the rivalry between the cities of León and Granada. This is the National Palace, facing Parque Central.

Parque Darío, in Managua, is named for poet Rubén Darío. City was almost destroyed by an earthquake in 1931, and the government was moved temporarily.

Club Managua is one of city's numerous impressive buildings. Beauty of the city is enhanced by its location on the southeast shore of 38-mile-long Lake Managua.

Ministry of Public Health, Managua, deals with a population that is principally of mixed Spanish and Indian extraction. The main agricultural crop is coffee.

Photos: National Tourist Board of Nicaragua

PANAMA CANAL IS "A DREAM OF CENTURIES COME TRUE"

An idea that occurred to the earliest Spanish explorers, the Panama Canal took many years to build and surpasses all other man-made waterways both in cost and in difficulty. It is 50.72 mil long from channel entrance in the Cari bean to deep water in the Pacific. Becau the canal runs generally southeast fro

Constant dredging is required to keep channels at proper depth. Landslides have sometimes blocked passage of the Gaillard cut, 8 miles long, 45 feet deep.

Ship's passengers have excellent view of the locks in action. Traffic moves in both directions, since all locks are double. Over 5,000 ships a year use canal.

Atlantic ports of Colón and Cristobal, the Pacific entrance is paradoxically miles east of the Atlantic one. Trip rough the canal takes 7 to 8 hours.

otos: A. L. Koolish

PANAMA IS A MINIATURE SPAIN

Fiestas, bullfights, colorful costumes and the gay nightlife of Panama City may make you think you're in Spain. By ship, Panama is 5 days from New York. By air, it's only 4½ hours from Miami.

Ruins of Cathedral in old Panama remind you of country's historic past, when it was route by which treasures the Inca empire were carried to Spai

Hotel Internacional, Panama City, has up-to-date facilities, old world charm.

Panama has Cabana Sun Club by pool, roof garden, air-conditioned rooms.

Panama City is near Pacific end of canal, is capital of Panama, industrial center.

Famous San Blas Indians make their home on the picturesque Mulatas Islands, near Cape San Blas, a point in north Panama which juts out into Caribbean.

San José, capital of Costa Rica, is a bustling city on main business street. **Airport at La Sabana, west of San José.**

Residential section has great charm, with many Spanish balconies and patios. **Even small towns have palatial churches**

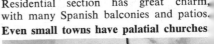

COSTA RICA: HEART OF THE AMERICAS

Located in the geographical center of the Americas, Costa Rica is a country of high culture, education, and political stability. Coffee is its principal crop. Air and steamer services are plentiful

Photos: Ewing Galloway; bottom left, Ace Williams (Black Star

Voyage 4
SOUTH AMERICA

Air travel makes it possible for you to make an extensive trip to South America even if you have just two weeks for a vacation. For example, Panagra's luxurious flight, *El Inter-Americano,* leaves Miami every night at eight and reaches Panama at midnight. It arrives in Lima, Peru, in time for breakfast, in Santiago, Chile, right after lunch. A mere twenty-five minutes takes you across the majestic Andes, then, speeding over the flat Argentine pampas, the flight touches down at Buenos Aires. If you prefer to start down the East Coast, Pan American will take you on *El Presidente,* a Super-6 Clipper flight, direct to Port of Spain, Trinidad, then on to Rio de Janeiro, Brazil, Montevideo, Uruguay, and Buenos Aires. Other air lines also serve the continent.

If you have time to travel by ship, that is the way for a vacation of real relaxation. Grace Line's two fine ships, *Santa Paula* and *Santa Rosa,* make 12-day cruises to Curaçao, La Guaira (permitting you to visit Caracas, Maracay and Lake Valencia), Puerto Cabello, Cartagena, and back to New York. Other Grace Line ships go through the Panama Canal and call at all the principal West Coast ports down to Chile. On the East coast, the Moore-McCormack

S.S. SANTA ROSA HAS DECK POOL.

Line, and the Argentine State Line (from New York), and the Delta Line (from New Orleans) take you to Rio, Santos, Montevideo and Buenos Aires. Round trip from New York to Buenos Aires takes about 38 days.

As to climate, South America can offer almost everything. Near the equator, the lowlands and coastal regions have tropical climate, but the high mountain regions are surprisingly cool. Below the equator, countries in the temperate zone have moderate climate with four seasons reversed from those we are used to in North America.

Spanish is the official language of all the South American countries except Brazil, where some 45 million people speak Portuguese. In all the well-traveled centers, however, English is spoken. A short course in Spanish or Portuguese, or at least a phrase book, may add to the comfort and interest of your travels South.

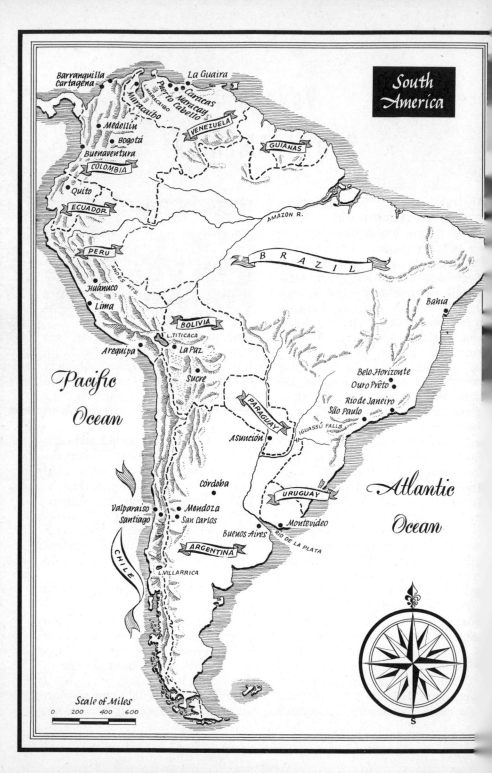

BOLIVAR AND THE ANDES DOMINATE VENEZUELA

NEW AUTOPISTA HIGHWAY, LA GUAIRA TO CARACAS, COST $70,000,000.

Simon Bolivar was born in Caracas, 1783. Now, more than a hundred years after his death, the people remember with awe and reverence "the great Liberator" who freed Venezuela and five other countries and ended Spanish power in South America. The fabulous human career of Bolivar is matched by a stupendous natural phenomenon, the great *cordillera* of the Andes flowing from Venezuela 4,600 miles south.

Photo: Hamilton Wright

Venezuela

Capitol building's most famous room is the Salon Eliptico, with heroic paintings.

The Pantheon is the "Westminster Abbey" of Caracas, with tombs of national heroes.

Center of Caracas is Plaza Bolivar, with statue of Liberator, important buildings.

"Casa Natal," birthplace of Bolivar, has become a national shrine, with mementos.

Cathedral is one of impressive buildings of old Spanish city, with narrow streets.

Country club has swimming pool, golf course, view of surrounding mountains

132

Photos: Grace Line; center left, Richard Joseph; bottom right, Hamilton Wright

Altamira is one of several new residential sections of Caracas, with broad boulevards.

The city is in a hollow, with the mountains towering around it on every side.

8-story twin sky-scrapers overlooking Centro Bolivar will house government offices when finished. Beneath the Centro lies a bus station, parking space for autos.

Photos: Hamilton Wright

133

Venezuela

"Virgen del Valle" is patron saint of Island of Margarita, 15 miles off coast.

Lake Maracaibo is fabulous source of oil wealth. 2600 derricks spread 36 miles.

Hotel Jardin in Maracay was designed by French architect in Algiers manner.

Angel Falls, 3,212 feet, world's highest, is in Gran Sabana, seen by few whites

Maracaibo is thriving city of 150,00 in oil district. This is Government House

134

Winding 12,000 feet high through the northern chain of the Andes, this highway connects Venezuela and Colombia, is only link with 30 towns on western slope.

Hotel Tamanaco, in Caracas, is 400-room $8,000,000 hostelry with huge outdoor swimming pool, sweeping terraces, a gay patio, and attractive tropical gardens.

Maiquetía Airport, right on the coast at La Guaira, is the terminus for Caracas.

Grace Line's sleek ships dock regularly at La Guaira, Venezuela's main sea gate.

Rio de Janeiro's trade-mark is 1,296-foot Sugar Loaf Mountain, guarding the entrance to Guanabara Bay. The summit is reached by aerial railroad, has fine views.

Photo: A. L. Koolis

BRAZIL'S CITIES DEFY WILDERNESS

Brazil, covering almost half the land area of South America, is larger than the continental United States and is exceeded in size only by the U.S.S.R., China and Canada. Most of the country is vast, untamed wilderness, but its pioneers have carved out some of the world's most interesting cities, fabulous Rio de Janeiro, modern São Paulo, and the port of Santos.

Copacabana Beach is the promenade spot of Rio, like the Champs-Elysées in Paris.

Praça Paris is one of Rio's bayside parks, its formal gardens unsurpassed in world.

Mosaic sidewalks, palm-lined boulevards make walking pleasant for Rio's citizens.

Palatial residences like this testify to wealth of fashionable Avenida Beira Mar.

Brazil

Ride from Rio to Petrópolis is over mountain road scarcely matched in the world.

Luxurious Quitandinha Hotel was scene of the 1947 Inter-American Conference.

Coffee is Brazil's leading export. Much of the work of processing is done by hand.

Carnival, held each year before Lent brings out weird costumes, much gaiety

Ouro Prêto, originally gold-rush town, is treasure house of baroque architecture.

Belo Horizonte is "planned city" laid o in 1895 along lines of Washington, D.

Photos: Charles Perry Weim top left, Pan American World Airw

Crowded fishermen's harbor of Salvador is spiderweb of sails. The city was founded as São Salvador da Bahia de Todos os Santos, has since been known as Bahia.

Salvador's landmark is this 234-foot elevator between lower and upper town.

Iguassú Falls, on Brazil-Argentina border, are higher, wider than Niagara, drop 210 feet.

Brazil

São Paulo boasts a 22-story library. You will find familiar magazines on the stands.

Business buildings in São Paulo, "world fastest growing city," suggest Hollywoo

São Paulo's great avenues have under-passes and viaducts to speed traffic. The

Triangulo at heart of city is much lik Chicago's Loop. Population is 2,600,000

URUGUAY, WITH ITS FAMOUS BEACHES, IS PLAYGROUND OF SOUTH AMERICA

Smallest, but one of most progressive of South American nations, Uruguay is often compared to Denmark and to Switzerland, and its renowned beach area is known as "the Riviera of South America." Uruguay is about size of New England. It was claimed by both Portuguese and Spanish. After the wars of independence, it emerged as a buffer state between Brazil and Argentina and was recognized by foreign powers in 1828. Uruguayans make no attempt to match power with their larger neighbors, but concentrate on earning a living—largely from agriculture—and on making their country a well-run republic with a deep belief in democracy.

Plaza Independencia, on Montevideo's main artery, features statue of national hero, José Gervasio Artigas. Calle Sarandi leads downtown, Avenida 18 de Julio up.

Uruguay

Another view of Plaza Independencia shows the modern Victoria Plaza Hotel.

Skyscraper Palacio Salvo contains Hotel Palacio Salvo, with 10th fl. dining room.

La Carreta monument in the Parque de los Aliados (Park of the Allies) represents the spirit of undiscourageable pioneering. Done in bronze, it is wonderfully real.

Avenida 18 de Julio takes name from date of Uruguay's proclamation of freedom.

Avenida Agraciada, lined with beautiful buildings, leads to Legislative Palace.

Photos: Oficina Nacional de Turismo de Uruguay; top right and center, A. L. Koolis

Distinctive modern apartment has
flamboyant exterior decoration.

Playa Carrasco is just outside city limits of
Montevideo. The beach has an immense casino.

Music, dancing and gaiety feature
the annual Montevideo carnival.

Playa Pocitos is another in the string of famous beach resorts that surround Montevideo.

Punta del Este is one of the top
sea resorts of all South America.

Legislative Palace, containing 30 kinds of marble,
is matched in splendor only by Cuba's *Capitolio*.

ARGENTINA BOASTS MIGHTY METROPOLIS

Buenos Aires, the "City of Fair Breezes," is as cosmopolitan a city as any in the world. It is largest in South America, with population of nearly three million, and covers 80 square miles. It offers theaters, opera, concerts. There's a modern subway system, hundreds of trams and thousands of busses. Café-sitting has developed almost to the point it has in Paris. In spite of strange new winds, Buenos Aires can be a place to have a lot of fun.

Palermo Park has fine rose gardens, statue of Carlos María de Alvear, hero of revolution.

Argentine National Congress building faces Congress Plaza, with monu-

Luxurious Plaza Hotel faces Plaza San Martín, is well known to North American visitors.

Plaza de Mayo is in the heart of old Buenos Aires. Directly across

144

Photos: Copyright, Charles Perry Weimer two in center of spread, Panagra

ments and fountains that recall the grand manner of European capitals.

Kavanaugh Building is second tallest in South America. Alvear Palace Hotel is next door.

ou see the dusty-pink Casa Rosada Pink House), residence of President.

Subway stations (entrance above) have artistic tile work depicting scenes in Argentine life.

Teatro Colón, municipal opera house, seats 3500 and is one of best equipped in world.

Argentina

Mendoza (San Martín monument above) is wine and fruit center, "Garden of Andes."

Córdoba, 400 miles northwest of Buenos Aires, is noted for beautiful Cathedral.

Gauchos are more colorful than U.S. cowboys. Pampas cover 200,000 square miles.

Hotel Llao-Llao (pronounced by Argentines Jao-Jao, with the "j" soft as in French) is most famous of the mountain inns in the Lake District, near Chile

Monte Tronador is an Andean peak of 11,200 feet, with number of waterfalls and glaciers. Nearby is Swiss-settled San Carlos de Bariloche, like Alpine village.

Spectacular Nahuel Huapí National Park, in Argentine Lake district, is one of most scenic regions in all Latin America. It's a thousand miles west of Buenos Aires.

147

PARAGUAY IS OFF BEATEN TRACK

Paraguay and Bolivia are South America's two wholly inland countries. Paraguay's Asunción (founded Assumption Day, 1536) has a strong lure for travelers who are fed up with big cities. It is thoroughly primitive, and thoroughly charming.

Asunción may be reached easily by air, or by 4-day voyage by river steamer from Buenos Aires, up Paraná and Paraguay. Lace made at Itaguá village is famous.

Asunción Palace is newest hotel. Gran Hotel del Paraguay was once residence.

You'll often see countrywomen riding market, sitting side-saddle on donkey

Photos: Ewing Gallow

CHILE'S MOUNTAINS STRETCH 2,600 MILES

INDIAN PONCHOS SHOW YOU THIS IS NOT SWITZERLAND BUT CHILE.

veraging barely 110 miles in width, Chile a narrow strip extending from Peru wn to the tip of South America, a disnce greater than that from New York Los Angeles. Within a short distance of the coast the formidable Andes rise to some of the hemisphere's highest peaks. The Chilean lake district, with 12 lakes all differing in the color of their water, offers magnificent scenery, great sport.

oto: Pan American World Airways

Chile

The Alameda, in Chile's capital of Santiago, is also known as Avenida Bernardo O'Higgins, named for one of the patriots who led the movement for independence.

Hotel Puyehue, famed hot springs resort, is among most sumptuous in South America.

In a Chilean rodeo, *huasos* are judged by speed and accuracy in stopping steer

Golf Club at Los Leones: Sports in Chile take precedence over almost everything.

Club Hípico in Santiago, offering horse racing, is one of show places of continen

150

Photos: Grace Line; center left, Pan American World Airways; bottom left, Pan American-Grace Airways; bottom right, Panag

Valparaiso, most important port on west coast of South America, is terminus of the Transandine Railroad to Argentina. City is bounded by hills, reached by funiculars.

Pucón on Lake Villarrica is outstanding resort, dominated by snowy volcano.

Valparaiso attracts tourists to its nearby beaches, like Playa Torpederas (above).

Photos: A. L. Koolish; bottom left, Grace Line; bottom right, Panagra

151

Chile

The famed statue of Christ the Redeemer marks Argentina-Chile border in Andes.

Nearby Portillo is ski center of Chile, with eight-story hotel, trails, lifts, runs.

Viña del Mar is Chile's outstanding sea resort, with its backdrop of snowy Andes.

Name means "Vineyard of the Sea" and it's a center for fruit, wine and vegetables.

Photos: Pan American-Grace Airways; top right, Grace Line

BOLIVIA'S LA PAZ IS HIGHEST BIG CITY IN WORLD

At an altitude of 11,909 feet, La Paz is the highest large city in the world, with 320,000 residents living more than two miles above sea level. Some say it's the world's highest capital, but accurate research indicates that Lhasa, Tibet, is slightly higher, although it is a comparatively small place with only 20,000 population. Then too, La Paz is not the legal capital of Bolivia (Sucre is), but La Paz developed more rapidly because of better transportation and has been since 1900 the actual seat of the government. Nearest seaport is Mollendo, in Peru.

Lake Titicaca is largest lake in South America and highest large lake in world.

Prado is the main boulevard of La Paz. Visitors often find high altitude hard to get used to at first; it is advisable to take cabs for sightseeing rather than walk.

Bolivia

One of main streets of La Paz is Avenida 16 de Julio. At left is office of Patino

Mines, fabulous enterprise that put Bolivia 3rd among world producers of tin

Cathedral at La Paz, on Plaza Murillo, is one of largest churches in South America.

Equestrian statue of General Antonio José de Sucre is prominently located

154

Puerta del Sol, "Gateway of the Sun," leads to pre-Inca ruins at Tiahuanaco.

A visit to the Indian market in La Paz is a must, for a look at cholo costumes.

Sucre, seat of the nation's supreme court, is the center of old Spanish culture.

rata is charming resort town, once important gold-mining center. Working of the mines has recently been resumed. 90% of Bolivia's exports are minerals.

This mountain valley is near Huánuco, reached by rail, crossing 15,000 ft. passes.

PERU IS QUEEN OF WEST COAST

Lima, capital of Peru, is one of the world's most fascinating cities. A mixture of Indian and Spanish tradition, it is gay and sophisticated. It's a spectacular country physically: the narrow strip along the coast, the stupendous Andes, the Amazon lowlands. The road from Lima up the Andes rises 15,948 feet in 85 miles!

Torre Tagle Palace in Lima is a beautiful survival of seventeenth-century design.

Cornerstone of the Cathedral, on Plaz de Armas, was laid by Francisco Pizarro

Peruvian folk dancers exhibit their gay costumes. February has 3-day carnival.

October is month of annual Fair. And Memorial stands before Fair Groun

156

In Lima's streets, advertising signs contrast with dignified Spanish buildings.

Lima's shops are good place to buy silver, leather, antiques and Incan curiosities.

Church of San Marcello, an excellent example of Spanish style, was built in 1584.

Arequipa, in the south, is a picturesque city. This is the Church of San Augustin.

oya Indians (Peru's population has 3 llion Indians) sell silver and baskets.

Machu Picchu ruins, amazing Inca city, weren't discovered by white men till 1911.

tos: A. L. Koolish; center, Pan American
ld Airways and Pan American-Grace
ways; bottom left, Copyright, Charles
y Weimer; bottom right, Grace Line

COLOMBIA HAS COLOR, CULTURE

Colombia, perhaps the most purely Spanish of all South American nations, is a country of infinite variety and color. In Bogotá, its isolated mountain capital, there are more bookshops than cafés, and the city is frequently referred to as the "Athens of America." Its theaters are very fine and there is an excellent conservatory of music and a national orchestra. Orchids grow in wild profusion in Colombia and are one of the principal sights in Cali and Medellín. Colombia is only South American country which fronts on both Atlantic and Pacific.

Parque Nacional is largest, most beautiful park in Bogotá, with extensive gardens, promenades.

Bell Tower of the San Felipe Fortress, Cartagena, gave warning of enemy ships.

Circo de Santamaria, in Bogotá, is or of world's greatest bull-fighting ring

Cartagena is one of oldest cities in the Western Hemisphere, founded 1533. It be- came "treasure city" of the Spanish Ma where conquistadores kept their spo

158

Swimming pool of the Del Prado Hotel, Barranquilla, is a favorite tourist spot.

Medellín is Colombia's leading industrial city, center of the rich gold-mining area.

A visitor picks orchids growing wild in jungle near Buenaventura, a leading port.

Cali is old colonial city with eight fine parks, churches, magnificent haciendas.

Puente Roman in Cartagena is the bridge which joins the city with island of La

Manga, one of main residential sections. Principal beach resort nearby is Marbella.

Photos: Grace Line; top left, Intercontinental Hotels; bottom, Foto Mangini

ECUADOR CLAIMS OLDEST CITY OF THE NEW WORLD

Quito, capital of Ecuador, makes what may prove a valid claim to being oldest city in Western Hemisphere. Once occupied by the Quitu Indians, it was captured in the 15th century by the Incas.

Plaza de Independencia, in Quito, is flanked by Cathedral and Government Palace. Quito, under Spanish till 1822 joined Gran Colombia, then broke away

Guayaquil is largest city of Ecuador and its principal seaport, about 60 miles from ocean on the Guayas River.

Simple monument marks the Equatorial Line in Ecuador

Voyage 5
GREAT BRITAIN AND IRELAND

Going by an English ship—Cunard's great *Queen Mary, Queen Elizabeth, Mauretania, Caronia* or one of the others—is perhaps the best introduction to Britain because you're surrounded by English tradition and atmosphere as soon as you step aboard. But there are plenty of delightful ways to get to England. Some ships put you off by tender at Plymouth, others dock at Liverpool, many at the great port of Southampton for the short train ride to London. If you're going to Ireland, take a ship that lands you at Cobh.

Flying across the Atlantic has its delights too. You can go direct to Shannon, for Ireland, or to Glasgow for Scotland, or to London Airport.

When you get there, hiring one of the easy-to-manage English cars is an excellent way to get about because the distances are so short. You'll readily get used to driving on the "wrong" side of the road, and you'll find many charming places for "tea" and for overnight stops. If you prefer, England is well covered by the British Railways network, and there are good bus lines. Most distances are too short for air travel, but the plane from London to Dublin avoids a possibly rough crossing of the 130-mile-wide Irish Sea.

The greatest appeal of England to many Americans is the great abun-

S.S. CARONIA LEAVES NEW YORK

dance of historic "things you've heard about" . . . Shakespeare's Stratford, the great mystery of Stonehenge, Westminster Abbey, the Houses of Parliament and Big Ben, the Tower of London, the Lake Country beloved of the poets, changing of the guard at Buckingham Palace, Peter Pan in Kensington Gardens, and Eros in Piccadilly. With the accession to the throne of young Elizabeth II, royalty takes on new glamor. Theater is at its best in London, and there are music, art, golf and other sports.

England is but 500 miles long, and so narrow that it is nowhere possible to be as much as one hundred miles from the sea. The climate, affected by the Gulf Stream, is temperate.

All in all, with its many differences, England offers a common language and the closest thing to home that you will find anywhere abroad . . . a great common heritage.

Great Britain and Ireland

LONDON

1 TOWER BRIDGE
2 TOWER OF LONDON
3 BUCKINGHAM PALACE
4 PICCADILLY CIRCUS
5 TRAFALGAR SQUARE
6 BRITISH MUSEUM
7 ST. PAUL'S CATHEDRAL
8 WESTMINSTER ABBEY
9 HOUSES OF PARLIAMENT

HYDE PARK
GREEN PARK
ST. JAMES'S PARK
THAMES RIVER

Atlantic Ocean

North Sea

SCOTLAND

Inverness

TROSSACHS
LOCH LOMOND

Glasgow   Edinburgh

GIANT'S CAUSEWAY

Londonderry
NORTHERN IRELAND
Belfast

Durham

LAKE DISTRICT
Windermere

York

Irish Sea

IRELAND

Dublin

ARAN ISLANDS

SHANNON R.

Llandudno   Liverpool
Rhyl   Chester
Caernarvon

ENGLAND

Norwich
Ely
Cambridge

WALES

Aberystwyth

Stratford-on-Avon

Colchester

Oxford
COTSWOLD HILLS   THAMES R.   London

Salisbury   Canterbury

Brighton

Exeter

ISLE OF WIGHT

English Channel

FRA

Scale of Miles
0   20   60   100

OVERS SIT BY THE THAMES, ON TOWER WALK, BESIDE THE BRIDGE.

oto: Henri Cartier-Bresson (Magnum)

FROM DOME OF ST. PAUL'S CATHEDRAL YOU LOOK OVER THE THAMES, THE BUSTLING, SMOKY CITY OF LONDON, HEART OF COMMONWEALTH.

Photo: Henri Cartier-Bresson (Magnum)

Westminster Abbey has been the setting for the coronation of English monarchs from the year 1066, which saw the crowning of Harold II, last of the Saxon kings, and William the Conqueror, down to the recent coronation of Elizabeth II. The Abbey, officially called *Collegiate Church* *of St. Peter in Westminster,* is one of the finest examples of Early English architecture in England. Poets' Corner (Longfellow is the only American poet included is one of the high spots for visitors. Another is Henry VII's magnificent chapel The third is the old Coronation Chair

Photo: British Travel Association

Buckingham Palace is residence of the Royal Family in London. When the Queen is there, the changing of guard ceremony takes place every other day at 10:30 a.m.

The Houses of Parliament, by the Thames, with Big Ben in the tower make the most celebrated landmark in England. Probably you've heard chimes of Big Ben by radio.

St. James's Palace was built by Henry VIII in 1532. Changing of the guard ceremony takes place here when Que is not in residence at Buckingham Palac

10 Downing Street is the home of Prime Minister, equivalent of U.S. White House.

Chelsea Arts Ball at Royal Albert Hal New Year's Eve, is England at its gayes

The Tower Bridge spans the Thames just below the Tower of London. The great towers, joined by latticed footbridges, make it most impressive of the bridges.

Crown Jewels, on display in the Tower, include the biggest diamond in existence.

Tower of London, guarded by the famous Beefeaters, is a "must" for all visitors.

The Orb of England and the Queen's Orb are among historic regalia in the display.

Photos: British Travel Association; bottom left, A. Milton Runyon

St. Paul's Cathedral, Renaissance master-piece of Sir Christopher Wren, stands on summit of Ludgate Hill, a landma͘ for miles. Visit the "whispering gallery

Photo: British Travel Associati

Hyde Park has an area of 361 acres. Together with Kensington Gardens it makes a continuous park of more than 600 acres, favorite place for mass meetings.

Crowds of workers cross London Bridge on foot or by bus, on way to their shops and offices. Peak hour for the thousands of travelers is from 8:30 to 9:15 a.m.

Photos: British Travel Association; bottom, Henri Cartier-Bresson (Magnum)

Trafalgar Square, seen through terrace columns of the National Gallery, is a favorite site for political demonstrations. On south side towers Nelson Monument

Library in the House of Lords contains works of legal and historical character.

Chamber of the House of Commons, rebuilt in same style after 1941 bombing.

The British Museum is unrivaled for the variety of its exhibits, Elgin Marbles, Rosetta Stone, one of four copies of the Magna Charta, four-million-book library.

Photos: British Travel Association

Ceremony of Trooping the Color is held at the Horse Guards Parade, Whitehall.

When you've lost your car, or your way, ask the policeman at Piccadilly Circus.

Madame Tussaud's Exhibition of Wax-works attracts many visitors including the

Pan American stewardess shown her looking at the tableau of Henry VII

Photos: William E. Reinhardt, Jr.; to right, Henri Cartier-Bresson (Magnum bottom, British Travel Associati

iccadilly Circus is one of city's best-
nown features. It's a circle formed by
the junction of five streets. The statue
of Eros stands atop the central fountain.

Hampton Court Palace, for over two centuries a royal residence, was started in 1514 by Cardinal Wolsey. Visit celebrate Maze in the gardens, the picture gallery

The Knights of the Garter Procession enters St. George's Chapel, Windsor—a building of which it has been said, "Such perfection is scarcely of this world."

Through Henry VIII's gateway at Windsor Castle, we watch the royal guard.

The Town of Windsor is connected by bridges with Eton and Eton College.

Photos: British Travel Association; bottom left, A. Milton Runyon; bottom right, Charles Marschalek

England OXFORD

Oxford University has 21 colleges for men, 4 for women. It dates back to 12th century. High Street is known to Oxford grads all over the world as "The High."

Christ Church, familiarly known as "the House," is the largest college in Oxford.

Magdalen Tower, bell-tower of Magdalen College, is setting of May Morning Hymn.

The **"Backs"** are the lovely tree-shaded grounds on left bank of the River Cam.

Cambridge University, on the River Cam, is the other great seat of learning.

St. John's College, founded 1511, is one of the 20 colleges; 2 are for women.

On way to Cambridge, visit Audley End, palatial Jacobean Renaissance mansion.

Boating, or "punting," on the Cam is one of the delights of idyllic Cambridge.

Stratford-on-Avon was the birthplace, in 1564, of William Shakespeare. It attracts some 100,000 visitors a year, is near enough London for a day's visit.

Shakespeare's birthplace was originally part of a long row of terrace cottages.

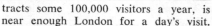

Anne Hathaway's cottage, birthplace of Shakespeare's wife, has thatched roof.

Shakespeare Memorial Theatre is large, modern, seems out of keeping with the rest of Stratford, but is well suited to fine presentation of bard's great plays.

This view from Warwick Castle indicates charm of this medieval baronial castle.

Tintern Abbey, founded by Cistercians in 1131, is now romantic, roofless ruin.

Photos: British Travel Association; bottom left, Richard Joseph

181

Canterbury, one of most revered shrines, has been called "The Mother City of the Anglo-Saxon Race." Splendid cathedral begun in 1070, was completed in 150?

Canterbury was stormed by Julius Caesar. War bombings uncovered Roman ruins.

Visitors to Canterbury pass through the city gates, follow route of pilgrims of old.

Mermaid Row in Rye is peaceful English scene that attracts visitors and artists.

Knole, one of finest baronial mansions, has 365 rooms, is now open to visitors.

Oast houses, these odd conelike structures in Penshurst, are used for drying hops.

Dover Castle was built in 12th century by Henry II. Nearby is Roman lighthouse.

Salisbury Cathedral is the most perfect realization of pure English Gothic, possibly because it was built in 38 years, with the 404-foot steeple added later.

Stonehenge, a mass of stones set on end, is one of Britain's greatest curiosities.

Druid ceremony at dawn on Midsummer Day is one of the rituals held regularly

Brighton, one hour by electric train from London, is England's largest and most famous seaside resort. Often crowded, it is referred to as "London by the Sea."

Winchester, with its red brick Georgian buildings, has true English personality.

Once capital of kingdom, Winchester is famous for its cathedral and its school.

The Isle of Wight is just off the south coast, below Southampton. The town of Ventnor, built on terraces above the sea, is one of the best-known health resorts.

Photos: Winchester by Richard Joseph; others by British Travel Association

Exeter, County town of Devon, has enough historic buildings to give you the feeling that it's one of the traditional centers of the lovely West of England.

Ancient Guild Hall in Exeter has pillared façade projecting over the sidewalk.

Royal Clarence Hotel, near Exeter Cathedral, has old-fashioned, quiet charm

Photos: Richard Josep

Clovelly, delightfully situated in a narrow rift in the cliffs of north Devon, descends in steps to a little cove. The picturesque houses have green trim.

Menabilly is home of Daphne du Maurier, author of *Jamaica Inn* and *Rebecca.*

Chapel of Gyllyngdune, in Falmouth, is said to be the smallest church in England.

In typical country "pubs" you'll find a darts game in progress most of the time.

English "pubs" have taken on many of the American "country store" qualities.

Photos: William E. Reinhardt, Jr.; center left, Doubleday; center right, Richard Joseph, bottom, Robert Capa (Magnum)

Fifteenth-century George Inn, Norton St. Philip, in Somerset, is called "the oldest licensed house in England." It's like hundreds of other country "pubs."

Somerset's lush fields make dairying a major industry. Its cheeses are famous.

Broadway, pretty village in Cotswold hills, is home of many artists, writers

Photos: Richard Josep

One of the show places of Hertfordshire is Hatfield House, Jacobean mansion built for Robert Cecil, Earl of Salisbury, Secretary of State to Queen Elizabeth.

he Norman town of Chepstow guards ye River. This gate is part of old wall.

Wye Valley is one of the most beautiful corners of Britain, with Forest of Dean.

Ely Cathedral dominates the treeless fens for miles around. The striking West Tower, except for its octagonal top and turrets, is of Transition Norman period.

In Tolleshunt D'Arcy is home of Margery Allingham, famous for mystery novels.

Norwich, capital of Norfolk, is an ancient city with many beautiful houses.

Photos: British Travel Association; bottom left, A. Milton Runyon; bottom right, Richard Jose

The Norfolk Broads, an area of shallow lagoons and placid streams, are near Norwich.

Colchester High Street was thoroughfare of the first Roman colony in Britain.

This gateway is all that's left of 11th-century Benedictine Abbey of St. John.

Norwich Mercury" is said to be oldest English paper still using original name.

Norwich Cathedral is majestic structure, with graceful, tapering 313-ft. spire.

York Minster is largest of England's medieval cathedrals. Its chief glory is its stained glass, contained in 120 windows. Most famous are West and "Five Sisters."

York has maze of narrow streets with names like Shambles (above), Gillygate, Whip-ma-whop-ma-gate. The city wall with four gates, are mostly 14th centur

Photos: British Travel Associati

The Royal Scot, British Railways' famous express, ascends Shap Fell, Westmoreland, the longest gradient and highest point on the run between London and Scotland.

Hadrian's Wall, seen here at Housesteads, was built by Romans in second century.

Haworth, Yorkshire, was the Vicarage home of the celebrated Brontë family.

Durham Cathedral contains coffin of St. Cuthbert, carried on famous wanderings.

Harrowgate, high on Yorkshire moors, in center of England, is a beautiful resort.

The Anglican Cathedral at Liverpool is one of the most modern churches, under construction since 1904. When completed it will be the fourth largest in the world

Liverpool has 6 miles of docks. Several of transatlantic ships land you there.

The swashbuckling John of Gaunt bu one of the gateways in Lancaster Cast

Photos: British Travel Associat

Chester, with its well-preserved walls, is most medieval-looking town in England.

Steps give easy access to the walls, and you can walk along them for two miles.

"The Rows" are unique Chester feature: arcades, built high to avoid muddy roads.

They form continuous passage from shop to shop without going down to the street.

Ullswater, second in size, is said to be grandest of the English lakes in scenery.

Buttermere is one of the smaller lakes. There are 16 lakes, in 35 square miles.

Windermere, the largest lake, is ten miles long, so narrow it looks like a river.

Hugh Walpole set his Herries saga here home also of Keats, Shelley, Wordsworth

Photos: British Travel Association; bottom, Richard Jose

The hamlet of Seatoller is one of the charming Cumberland villages that are best appreciated on a walking tour. Make your headquarters at a place like Keswick.

Grasmere, one of Lakeland's loveliest, was for 14 years the home of William Wordsworth. Visit Dove Cottage, where he lived, and the Wordsworth Museum.

Eton boys: You tell their standing by whether their collars are "turned down."

At Epsom Downs, the "Derby" and "Oaks" attract the fashionable crowds

Chimney sweep of Lancaster might have stepped right out of a Dickens' novel.

Oxford student is one of 8,000 undergra There are 590 teachers, called fellow

Photos: British Travel Assoc
tion; top right, Richard Jose

DAILY CHANGING OF THE GUARD AT EDINBURGH CASTLE IS COLORFUL.

SCOTLAND MEANS HILLS AND HISTORY

When you talk of Scotland, some people think of Bobbie Burns, some think of Mary, Queen of Scots, and some of Ben Hogan's victory at Carnoustie. For Scotland is a land of great diversity, of great cities like Edinburgh and Glasgow, of hills and lochs, of poets and novelists and golfers, of unwavering national pride.

oto: Richard Joseph

From Scott Monument in Princes Street, Sir Walter's statue looks across the city. The climb to the top is 287 steps, but you get a magnificent view on four sides.

Princes Street forms a valley down the middle of Edinburgh. On one side is old town, from great rock of Edinburgh castl to Holyroodhouse. Other side is new cit

Photos: British Travel Associati

At Holyrood Palace tragic Mary, Queen of Scots, lived and ruled during 16th century. Old town between the castle and palace is called the Royal Mile.

Behind the National Gallery looms the great Castle Rock. From castle battlements you get a superb view of the city and the Forth River in the distance.

Scotland

Glasgow is the largest city in Scotland and the second largest in Great Britain.

Biggest Glasgow industry is shipbuilding. John Brown's built Cunard's two *Queens*.

Loch Lomond, 23 miles long, is "Queen of the Scottish Lochs." Trossachs tour takes you between Glasgow and Edinburgh by Loch Lomond, Loch Katrine

Abbotsford is Sir Walter Scott's estate, across from the tweed-milling town of Galashiels, south of Edinburgh. Scott lived in this baronial mansion till 1832.

Loch Lomond steamer heads north from Inversnaid, between bonnie, bonnie banks.

The Forth Bridge, near Edinburgh, a mile long, took seven years to build, in 1880's.

Photos: British Travel Association; bottom left, Alleyne M. Runyon

Scotland

Dancing is an important part of Scottish gatherings, where kilted males compete.

Skirl of bagpipes is a familiar sound. Reed wind instruments' origin is unknown.

If you come by ship direct to Scotland, tender takes you up Clyde to Glasgow.

Bagpipe band celebrates the arrival of *Britannic.* You won't forget eerie sound

Photos: British Travel Association; Alleyne M. Runyon; bottom, Richard Joseph

Ballater (above) and Braemar (scene of Highland games) are in Aberdeen, north- east Scotland. Here you'll find the men who go after herring, salmon, whitefish.

Glamis Castle, ancestral home of Queen Elizabeth II and birthplace of Princess Margaret, is twelve miles north of Dundee. It probably dates from the 11th century.

The Falls of Leny are in a narrow moun- tain pass, northwest of Callander, tourist center for Trossachs and Loch Katrine, setting of Scott's *The Lady of the Lake.*

Scotland

Inverness is northernmost large town in Britain, good base for touring Highlands.

The Castle stands on the supposed site of castle where Macbeth killed Duncan.

Ross and Cromarty is one of northern counties, above Inverness, and across straits from Isle of Skye. Heather and hills make for beautiful grouse-hunting.

CAERNARVON CASTLE WAS KEY FORTRESS IN THE WELSH CAMPAIGNS.

WALES IS LAND OF COAL, CONTRAST

If you read *How Green Was My Valley* by Richard Llewellyn, or saw the picture, you have some idea of this land of twisting roads, craggy mountains, of hardworking, song-loving people. You won't forget the beauty of Welsh choral singing when you've heard it in a country chapel. Song climax is annual Eisteddfod.

Wales

Llandudno is a beach town on a peninsula at the northern tip of Wales. Planned a

Elan Valley reservoir at Aberystwyth is in one of many green valleys of Wales.

Aberystwyth is west coast's big resort, with castle on rock jutting out to sea.

Photos: British Travel Association

century ago, and laid out beautifully, it has mountains of Snowdonia as backdrop.

Welsh children turn out in their gayest costumes for Eisteddfod at Llangollen.

Good place for hiking is road from Barmouth to Dolgelley, where curfew rings.

St. David's Cathedral, Pembrokeshire, has none of Salisbury's lofty grace, but its low pitched roofs and square tower are in keeping with its bleak village. On the inside, the austerity changes to elaborate, almost Moorish ornamentation.

NORTHERN IRELAND GAVE THE U.S. TEN PRESIDENTS

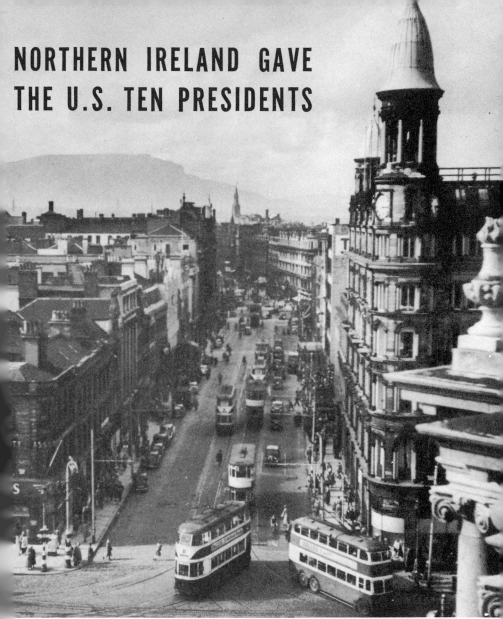

CITY HALL LOOKS DOWN DONEGALL PLACE, BELFAST'S MAIN STREET.

One reason why Northern Ireland will probably seem so familiar to you is that so many Ulster emigrants have come to the United States. Of the 33 men who have been Presidents, from George Washington to Dwight Eisenhower, at least ten are claimed to be of Ulster ancestry. Northern Ireland may be reached by boat or plane from Glasgow to Belfast, direct by plane from London. If you're coming up from Ireland, it's an easy trip by plane, train, bus or driving in your own car.

Photo: British Travel Association

Northern Ireland

Carrickfergus Castle is one of the best preserved Norman castles in the world.

There's wild country, and farmlands with hedges dividing them into tiny tracts.

Northern Ireland Parliament Buildings are situated atop hillside at Stormont.

Stormont Castle houses Prime Ministe and certain departments of government

Fair Head is the most northerly point in County Antrim. Nearby is the interesting

Ballygalley Castle Hotel, a part of whi dates back as far as the 17th centur

Photos: British Travel Assoc tion; top right, Richard Jose

he Giant's Causeway is the greatest
enic attraction in Northern Ireland.

Legend says these great basalt rocks once
formed causeway across sea to Scotland.

oto: British Travel Association

213

Northern Ireland

Dunluce Castle is near Portrush and Port Stewart which have wonderful beaches.

Londonderry City is 75 miles from Belfast. This is Shipquay Gate, Guild Hall.

Bangor, County Down, is historic town that has become a favorite sea resort.

Belfast Castle is one of city's many sights: Art Gallery, Museum, University.

Because it has a seacoast of 245 miles and many rivers, lakes and tideways, Northern Ireland has an abundance of boating, and some magnificent fishing

Photos: British Travel Association; bottom, Richard Joseph

IRELAND INVITES YOU TO "COME BACK TO ERIN"

We mentioned the number of emigrants who had come from Northern Ireland to the U.S.A., and that's probably even more true of Ireland itself. As you walk down the street, you'll often think you recognize someone, because the second, third and fourth cousins in America look just like the folks back home. You'll find Ireland a peaceful land whose pastoral scenes, green fields and hills, and soft mists will calm your nerves.

Getting to Ireland can be fun. Maybe you'll land at Cobh from your transatlantic steamer, or touch down in your plane at Shannon Airport, busiest center of international air traffic in the world. Gayest trip is from London on the Irish Mail, leaving London at tea time. About 11 p.m. you board a trim little ship at Holyhead, and sleep until you arrive at Dun Laoghaire, a few minutes from Dublin, the next morning. Or you can fly from London to Dublin by Aer Lingus.

All in all, you'll find St. Patrick's Island one of the friendliest nations to visit, even if you don't win a Sweeps!

O'CONNELL STREET SHOPPERS SET URBAN PACE UNIQUE IN IRELAND.

Photo: Fogra Failte

The Custom House, on the northern bank
of the River Liffey, between O'Connell

Bridge and the sea, was built in 17
from designs by James Gandon, Irelan

most gifted architect. One of Dublin's
finest public buildings, it ranks among

the most beautiful in Europe. Burned in
1921, it has been completely restored.

Photo: Fogra Failte

Ireland

An Tostal is Ireland's traditional festival, held each Spring. Here is a floral float passing the Presidential Dais and reviewing stand at the General Post Office.

Royal Dublin Society Horse Show is a high spot of the Dublin social season.

Arus Mhic Diarmuida is the ultra-moder bus terminal of Ireland Transport C

Photos: Fogra Fail

County Sligo combines with wild seacoast with rolling plains, mountains like Benweeskin.

Garravogue River drains Lough Gill into sea. On its south bank is town of Sligo.

Hunting to hounds is a most popular sport. These are Meath foxhounds, from north of Dublin. Other noted packs are Duhallow hounds, Tipperary foxhounds.

Photos: Fogra Failte

Ireland

Ireland's fertile fields and pastures occupy more than half nation's working people.

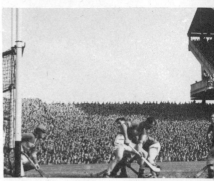

Tipperary plays Kilkenny in Hurling, an Irish national sport for 3,000 years.

"Lips that touch the Blarney stone will have the gift of gab," according to the Irish myth. Famous stone is at Blarne￼ Castle, is bussed by thousands annuall￼

Donegal is the northernmost county in Ireland. The region near Killybegs is known as "Finian's Country" because of its supposed role in *Finian's Rainbow*.

Benbulben, in County Sligo, is strange mountain that surges upward, then breaks off in a long, flat plateau. This is a rich area for the geologists and the botanists.

Shannon Airport has had over 200,000 passengers going through it annually, although longer-range planes may mean fewer stops at Shannon for refueling.

x

Ireland

Round tower, perfect after 1,000 years, tops Rock of Cashel, on Tipperary plain.

Muiredach Cross is most famed Celtic cross in world, with 22 sculptured panels.

Cashel of the Kings is Ireland's most noted group of ecclesiastical buildings.

This cottage in Sligo gives you a good idea of what Irish thatched roof is like

Irish folk dancing begins at early age, and it can be strenuous beyond belief!

Lisnabrin House, Curraghglass, is quiet charming country hostelry, in Waterford

222

landore, fishing village on a small inlet the Atlantic, in the southern part of County Cork, has a population of 82, is noted for its delightfully mild climate.

oto: Fogra Failte

Ireland

This Aran girl lives on Inishmore, one of 3 Aran Islands, 28 mi. west of Galway.

Aran Islanders are rugged; not as primitive as shown in movie, *Man of Aran*

Glendalough, County Wicklow, means Glen of the Two Lakes. Thackeray called it "sweet, wild and sad even in sunshine. Visit the 6th-century St. Kevin Monaste

Photos: Fogra Fo

Voyage 6
SCANDINAVIA

S.A.S. plane flies over northern Norway.

Clear-weather views from air are superb.

The Scandinavian countries are a geographical unit, joined by many ties of language, race and religion. And yet the several countries, Norway, Sweden, Finland, Denmark and Iceland, have many differences that make for delightful variety.

The first prehistoric cities of Scandinavia were founded by tall, blond Vikings who were not converted to Christianity until the year 1000. Wonderful relics of their early art are to be found in the museums of Oslo, Stockholm and Copenhagen.

Scandinavia is easily reached by air from the U.S. with good service by Scandinavian Airlines System and Pan American World Airways. Many flights offer free stopover privilege at Iceland. Swedish American Line's *Stockholm* and the luxurious new *Kungsholm* offer service from New York to Copenhagen and Gothenburg in 8 or 9 days. Norwegian America Line's trim *Oslofjord* and *Stavangerfjord* take you direct to Oslo in 9 days. From England, there is service both by sea and by air, and the same applies if you come from France or Benelux area. Fast express trains run to Copenhagen from Paris and other cities on the continent.

Shopping is delightful in Scandinavia for designers and craftsmen take great pride in their work. All the countries maintain permanent exhibits of arts and crafts, where you can examine them at leisure.

As a bookreader, you'll be especially interested in Scandinavian literature and in the many bookshops.

Photos: Scandinavian Airlines System; right, Konstantin Kostich

Arctic Ocean

ICELAND

Reykjavik

Miles 0 50 100

Atlantic
Ocean

U.S.S.R.

LAPLAND

Rovaniemi

LOFOTEN ISLANDS

SWEDEN

Trondheim

Gulf of Bothnia

FINLAND

Bergen

NORWAY

Oslo

Turku
Helsinki

Stavanger

Stockholm

GÖTA CANAL

Skagerrak

Kattegat

DENMARK

Aarhus

JUTLAND
Ribe

Odense

FYN

ZEALAND

Elsinore
Copenhagen

U.S.S.R.

Baltic Sea

GERMANY

POLAND

Scale of Miles
0 50 100 150 200

Scandinavia

N

S

In Henningsvaer Harbor, Lofoten Islands, nearly 1000 fishing boats moor for week end.

RUGGED NORWAY HAS MIDNIGHT SUN

Norway is a long, rangy country, with terrific distances, but you'll find the magnificent scenery worth the travel. People everywhere are friendly, from the cosmopolitan residents of Oslo to the Lapps of Nordland, "Land of the Midnight Sun." The fjords, deep inlets from sea, are nation's most spectacular sight.

Photo: Robert Capa (Magnum)

Across Oslo harbor, you see the new City Hall, inaugurated in 1950 during the city's 900th birthday celebrations. Fjord is the city's beautiful, sheltered harbor.

Statue of Henrik Ibsen, famous for his plays, stands before the National Theater.

Oslo University, founded 1811, has beautiful buildings. Also visit Nobel Institute

Oslo is modern in design, with planned business and residential neighborhoods.

"Karl Johans Gate" is the main business street, from station to Royal Palace.

Oslo's parks are famous. This is flower market, in the city. Holmenkollen, in hills behind town, gives a magnificent view. Frogner Park has the *Kon-Tiki* raft.

Norway

Oslo's Parliament is called the Storting. For many years, while Norway and Denmark were united, the city was called Christiania, after King Christian IV.

Akershus Castle was built about 1300 by Haakon V to protect Oslo against pirates. The royal residence from 1319 to 1380, it has fine view overlooking Oslo Fjord.

Sogne Fjord, 45 miles north of Bergen, is Norway's longest and deepest fjord, often called "King of the Fjords." Above is charming resort center of Balestrand

Photos: Norwegian National Trave Office; bottom, Konstantin Kostic

Nord Fjord is further north than Sogne Fjord. Both fjords are fed by glacial streams of mighty Jostedalsbre, largest ice field on the mainland of Europe.

Codfish hangs to dry in Lofoten Islands town of A, sometimes spelled Aa, and

formerly Aag. At left is tower used to spot salmon and trap them on the fjords.

Photos: Charles Marschalek; bottom right, Evans (Three Lions)

Norway

Geiranger Fjord is noted for the Pulpit, a rock promontory, Bridal Veil Falls.

Trondheim is Norway's 3rd city, seaport and gateway to north. This is market.

Bergen, Norway's 2nd largest city, has miles of docks, old Hanseatic buildings dating from early 16th century when the League dominated the commercial life

Jotunheim Mountains, in south central Norway, are popular for hiking. Legend says these majestic mountains, with 8,097 ft. peak, are home of "Jotuns," or giants.

Norwegian children might have stepped out of the pages of *"Leif the Lucky."*

Chair lift at Krokkleiva outside Oslo gives mountain climbing thrill easy way.

Heddel Stav church, Telemark, is one of thirty 700- to 900-year-old timber churches.

Market place at Stavanger: This 8th-century city is one of Norway's oldest.

Stockholm's many waterways and canals give it the title of "the Venice of the North." At top right is City Hall, mos[t] magnificent modern building in Europe

SWEDEN OFFERS A GAY VÄLKOMMEN!

Sweden has everything to attract th[e] tourist: it's the land of smörgåsbor[d] and wonderful things to eat; it share[s] marvelous scenery and such natural phe[-] nomena as the midnight sun with it[s] neighbor, Norway; and happy, vigorou[s] Swedes like visitors, make them welcome[.]

234

Photo: Swedish N[a]tional Travel Offic[e]

Royal Dramatic Theater saw debuts of Greta Garbo, Ingrid Bergman, others.

From gardens of City Hall, you see older area called "City between the Bridges."

Impressive Grand Hotel is located at the fashionable resort of Saltsjöbaden in the Stockholm archipelago, about one hour's trip from the center of the city.

"Golden Otter" Inn is one of the most famous of Swedish hotels. It is located at Granna on Lake Vatter, amid spectacular scenery of Sweden's Lake District

Photo: Swedish National Travel Offic

There are good beaches near Malmo, terminus of the ferry from Copenhagen.

55% of Sweden is forested; lumbering, pulp and paper are major industries.

Stockholm is the yachtsman's paradise. Pleasure craft outnumber the automobiles.

Photos: Swedish National Travel Office

Sweden

Fiddlers of Dalarna Province preserve charming customs and manner of dress.

St. Lucia's Day, December 13, is celebrated by girls wearing candle crowns.

Lapland extends across the northern end of Norway, Sweden, Finland, and north-

Sofia Girls demonstrate their grace and rhythm at Jubilee celebration in Town Hall gardens. Swedes love to keep fit.

Stout fishing boats put out into Baltic

west extremity of USSR. Mount Akka, in Swedish Lapland, is one of the most beautiful mountains in the country, with parts of it covered by eternal snows.

from Karlshamn port. Sport fishing is good.

Regattas in the Stockholm archipelago demonstrate skillful boat-handling of Swedish sailors, "born" with the knowledge.

Sweden

Arsta Railway Bridge, Stockholm, frames the modern Southern General Hospital.

View of Skeppsbron docks shows many boats that go to coastal points, Finland.

The Old City, also called "The City between the Bridges," is the oldest part of Stockholm. It retains much of its medieval character and has many notable building.

The Kvikkjokk region of Lapland, with many lakes, rivers, has rich vegetation.

Gota Canal offers charming steamer trip, 350 miles, Gothenburg to Stockholm.

Photos: Swedish National Trave
Office; top left, Uno Kabal
bottom right, Konstantin Kostich

THIS IS PARLIAMENT IN HELSINKI, "WHITE CITY OF THE NORTH."

FINLAND IS MODERN AND CORDIAL

Finland is known for its ultra-modern architecture, sunlit nights, beautiful scenery. Its people are blond, blue-eyed, and hospitable. If you want a vacation in an off-the-beaten-track country that offers some of the best facilities for comfort, your answer is Finland, a democratic republic that is ripe for discovery.

hoto: Finnish Na-
ional Travel Office

241

Helsinki Stadium, site of 1952 Olympic Games, shows sport-mindedness of Finns.

Although city is over 400 years old, it has largely been rebuilt in 20th century.

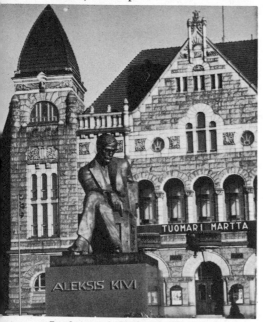

In front of National Theater is statue of Aleksis Kivi, 19th-century novelist.

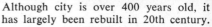

"Havis Amanda" statue symbolizes "The Maid Helsinki rising from the waters."

242

Photos: Finnish National Travel Office

Great Church is a composite architectural style with copper domes, Roman frontons.

President's Residence was Russian imperial palace in era of Grand Duchy.

National Museum houses large collections dealing with Finnish history and culture.

State University was founded in 1640 at Turku, transferred in 1828 to Helsinki.

Helsinki Central Station, built in 1919 by Saarinen, was partly burned in 1950.

City has three sheltered harbors, sometimes icebound in February and March.

Finland

Historic Turku, Finland's second largest city and former capital, until 1812, has a cathedral which was completed in 1290. Seaport is kept ice-free the year round.

This tall, severe 13th-century castle in Turku was enlarged during 16th century.

The straits between the Baltic and Gulf of Bothnia are dotted with many islands.

244

Photos: Finnish National Travel Office

Rovaniemi, capital of Finnish Lapland, is just south of the Arctic Circle. It is a winter-sports center and the trading and administrative center of that area.

Pallastunturi Inn, in Finnish Lapland, is good center for winter sports. There's skiing, hiking, hunting, salmon fishing. It's nearly 700 miles north of Helsinki.

Reindeer are frequent sight in Lapland; they pull a narrow sledge called *pulkka.*

Lapp newlyweds show colorful costumes, the men with white reindeer fur *peski.*

Photos: Finnish National Travel Office

Finland

Aulanko National Park is top resort and recreation area. This is Hotel Aulanko.

Olavinlinna Castle is in East Finland's lake region at summer spa of Savonlinna.

The Sauna, famous Finnish steam bath, is fixture of every home and of many hotels.

Vehoniemi Tourist Inn is a delightful stopping place in south central Finland.

From here you can go by water bu through lake regions to Aulanko Parl

Photos: Finnish N tional Travel Offi

COPENHAGEN'S DANISH RENAISSANCE TOWN HALL WAS BUILT IN 1894.

OR FRIENDLINESS, COME TO DENMARK

Among the predominant characteristics of Denmark are friendliness, flowers and song. The nation consists of the peninsula of Jutland and some 500 islands, including the large ones of Fyn and Zealand, the island that contains the capital city of Copenhagen, often called with good reason "the Paris of Scandinavia."

Photo: Danish National Travel Office

Gefion Fountain is at beginning of Langelinie, delightful walk beside the sea.

Statue of "The Little Mermaid" is based on one of Andersen's noted fairy tales.

The Tivoli is beautifully landscaped amusement park in the center of town, where you can hear symphony, dance, dine, attend famous pantomime theater

Photos: Danish National Travel Office

The Banqueting Hall in Christiansborg Castle is used by the King to receive in audience any of his subjects who have a problem or grievance to be discussed.

Church of Our Savior has an uncommon winding stairs on *outside* of the spire.

Frederiksborg Palace, in suburb of Copenhagen, now houses Historical Museum.

Palace of Amalienborg is the present royal residence, and the Changing of the Guard takes place there at noon dail with waving flags, fanfare of trumpe

Photo: Danish N
tional Travel Off

Silver is Denmark's top shopping attraction; Georg Jensen is most famous name.

Tivoli restaurants are good places to try the celebrated Danish smørrebrød.

At going-to-work time and quitting time a bicycle avalanche sweeps the streets.

As fresh hauls are brought in, fisherwomen clean them at quayside market.

The large sight-seeing motorboats that ply the canals take visitors past many of the most interesting parts of the city. Christiansborg Castle tower is at left.

Photos: Danish National Travel Office; top right, Konstantin Koch; center right, A. Milton Runyon

Denmark

Rosenholm Castle, in charming Jutland setting. is one of beautiful old castles.

Folk dances are performed at open-a Museum at Lyngby, near Copenhage

Archways of Christiansborg Castle glow with the lights of a midwinter evening.

Unobtrusive doorway on a Copenhag street opens to this lovely old courtya

Professor Olsen is one of the master designers of Royal Copenhagen Porcelain.

Hans Christian Andersen's charact live on in Royal Copenhagen figurin

252

Photos: Danish National Travel Off center, David Grunbaum, A. Milton Runy top right, bottom left, Konstantin Kos

In this little house in Odense, great story teller Andersen lived as a child.

Autumn sunshine gives mystic quality to impressive towers of Rosenborg Castle.

Round Tower at Regensen, built by King Christian V, now serves as observatory.

Odense, 3rd largest city of Denmark, has cathedral honoring Saint Canute.

Ribe is one of the fairytale towns of Denmark where storks nest on the roofs.

Denmark

Old town of Randers was important commercial center back in the Middle Ages.

Aarhus, Denmark's second city, has Town Hall that's ultramodern in architecture

Probably the smallest Town Hall in the world is to be found in Aebeltoft, Jut-

land, a fairytale town that dates from the 14th century. Noted for fisherie

Late autumn sunshine casts long shadows of strollers in Royal Square, Copenhagen.

The Jelling Runic Stone was erected year 980 by King Harald the Bluetoot

Photos: Danish National Travel Offi
top left, bottom left, David Grunba

Ancient guns guard Kronborg Castle, the "Elsinore Castle" of the play, *Hamlet*.

Children's Day celebration is one of the many expressions of Danish gaiety.

Kronborg Castle at Elsinore is the annual setting for the "Hamlet Festival."

From heights of the ramparts you can see the not-far-distant coast of Sweden.

Lovely Danish countryside is best seen slowly, traveling by bicycle or car. In

small town you may come across peasants and fishermen in charming old costumes.

Photos: Konstantin Kostich; center, Danish National Travel Office

Reykjavik, capital of Iceland, is chief port of nation, commercial and fishing center. Unique hot-water supply system, built 1945, utilizes natural hot springs.

Gullfoss gets its name of "Golden Fall" from double rainbow seen in its spray.

ICELAND IS ONE OF NEWER REPUBLICS

The first permanent settlement of Iceland was made in 874. The Althing, general assembly, was established in 930 and is the oldest legislative body in the world still in existence. After a referendum in 1944, the union with Denmark was ended and the new republic was proclaimed.

Average annual temperature at the capital ranges from 30° in January to 52° in July. Only about a quarter of the land is habitable, mainly the west, north and east coasts. Iceland is the westernmost state of Europe, 500 miles northwest of Scotland. It is completely "different," a magic, bewitching land

Photos: Ewing Galloway; bottom Hans Malmben (Black St

Voyage 7
EUROPE

Because we have reserved southern Europe for the Mediterranean Cruise section, this part covers France, the three Benelux countries, western Germany, Switzerland and western Austria. To get to this part of the continent from the United States, you are faced with the same happy dilemma: which way to travel? If you are of the school of thought that believes in stepping at once into the land of your choice, you can do so by boarding one of the foreign-flag carriers in New York. France offers the *Liberté, Ile de France* and *Flandre,* and the services of Air France. The Netherlands boasts the *Nieuw Amsterdam* and the smaller ships of Holland-America line, and KLM, the Royal Dutch Airlines. Switzerland and Belgium have no ships, but Swissair gives service of Swiss punctuality, and Sabena treats you royally on the way to Belgium.

On the way home, or on the way over, for that matter, you may want to try the superlative service that American lines offer. In ships, we have the great *United States* and proud *America.* And in the air, we rejoice in the dependability of Pan American World Airways and TWA Trans World Airline. Of course, you also have excellent service to the continent by Britain's great Cunarders which let you off at Le Havre

You travel in comfort on "Blue Train."

or Cherbourg. And BOAC connects with all air services.

When you arrive on the continent, there are travel choices, too. You may want to hire a car, as so many people are now doing. The railroads have many de luxe trains with romantic names, *Golden Arrow, Blue Train, Orient Express.* Busses are becoming increasingly popular, with good services like Europabus being able to take you by more attractive roads, and wait for you while you do your sightseeing. Quickest way to get from city to city on longer hauls is by air, either by one of the services mentioned above, or by British European Airways and Scandinavian Airlines which have very good continental networks.

Now turn the page for a preview, or postview, of your great journey.

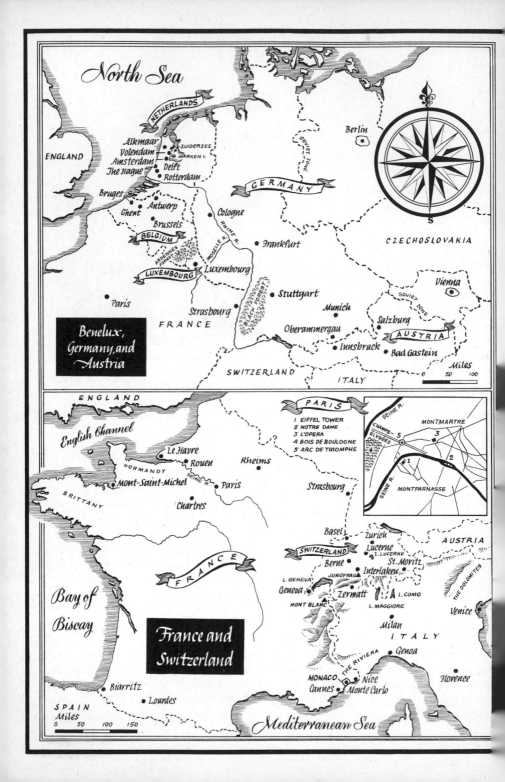

AMSTERDAM HAS 1,000 CANALS, MOST GOING DIRECTLY THROUGH CITY.

HOLLAND MEANS WINDMILLS, TULIPS

The Netherlands is a compact country, about one and a half times the size of Massachusetts. Because a quarter of the land is below sea level, as much as 21 feet, it has to be protected by dikes, windmills and electric pumps. Holland has picturesque old towns, villages that cling to old customs, and modern cities.

Glass-top passenger boat traverses the Amstel River. Dam on this river, from which city gets its name, was constructed in 13th century. City has 400 bridges.

Kalverstraat, with its many silversmiths, and Leidschestraat are shopping centers.

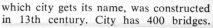

Rijksmuseum has fine Dutch and Flemish paintings, Rembrandt's *Night Watch*

Flower vendor displays her blooms beside Amsterdam's ancient Powder Tower.

Hotel L'Europe has steps at its front door giving easy access to the canal.

Royal Palace, on Dam Square, is not the Queen's home, is used for state affairs.

Amsterdam is a world-famous center for the cutting and polishing of diamonds.

Peace Palace at The Hague, built 1913, now houses the International Court of Justice under the UN. The Hague is one of the most beautiful cities of Europe.

Parliament Buildings: The Hague is not the capital, but is seat of government.

The Royal Family arrives at "Hall of Knights" for the opening of Parliament

Photos: Burton Holmes (Ewing Galloway); Netherlands National Tourist Office; Netherlands Information Service

Delft, five miles from The Hague, is one of the most typical old Dutch towns.

A center for ceramics, Delft sends its blue china and pottery all over world.

Rotterdam, principal Netherlands port, is rising anew from 1940 devastation.

On the lake at Sneek, northern Holland, many international regattas take place.

Netherlands

Scheveningen, fashionable sea resort near The Hague, has annual Music Festival.

Kampen is an ancient city with town hall, many buildings dating to 14th century.

Breda was site of treaty that gave New York and New Jersey colonies to British.

In Alkmaar, cheese market comes to life on Friday mornings, May to September.

Cheeses come to Alkmaar by barge, are unloaded by men with traditional garb.

Photos: Netherlands National Tourist Office bottom right, Netherlands Information Servic

Leiden is renowned for its University, founded 1575, and one of the most famous in Europe. City became printing center when Elzevir established his press.

Charming town of Franeker once boasted a university, suppressed by Napoleon.

This winter scene on Island of Marken might be straight out of *Hans Brinker*.

Photos: Netherlands National Tourist Office; bottom right, Netherlands Information Service

Netherlands

This is Holland: Windmill, canal with fisherman, boy and girl with flowers on the way to market.

In past 50 years, bulb-growing has become a major industry.

Volendam's costumes, picturesque houses attract many photographers and painters.

Holland's cattle is famous; the fertile polderland provides the best of grazing.

Photos: Konstantin Kostich; Netherlands National Tourist Office; Charles Marschalek; Netherlands Information Service

BELGIUM DISPLAYS MANY TREASURES FOR VISITORS

ANTWERP IS RIVALED ONLY BY ROTTERDAM AS TOP EUROPEAN PORT.

Belgium is a tiny country, 175 miles at its greatest length, but it is a tremendous treasure house of Flemish painting and Renaissance architecture. Here, oil painting began at least as early as in Italy. Another of Belgium's great tourist attractions is its forty miles of fine beaches, with resorts like Spa, Ostend and Knokke-LeZoute. Still another magnet is green beauty of Ardennes forest.

Fortress-like Steen is one of the few traces left of medieval Antwerp. Parts date back to the 10th century; during 13th century the castle was a prison.

Not all windmills are in Holland. This impressive one is on the way to Ghent.

Fountain of the Nymphs stands in front of Antwerp's late Gothic guild houses.

Cathedral of Notre Dame, Antwerp's incomparable Gothic structure, was built in 14th and 15th centuries, has 400-ft. spire. Contains several Rubens paintings.

Center of Brussels is *Grand' Place,* site of original 10th century settlement. Here are situated Town Hall (above), begun in 14th century, and medieval guildhalls.

Arcade Cinquantenaire opens on a park and connects two galleries, one containing military antiquities, the other an art collection with rare ivories, enamels.

Brussels, capital of Belgium, is center of country's banking and commercial life, and one of Europe's richest, most beautiful cities. Town square has flower stalls.

Ghent is main city of East Flanders, has 10th century cathedral, old guildhalls.

Bruges (right) is Flemish for bridges; more than 50 cross the canals of this famed medieval town dating from the 7th century. Caxton learned printing here.

Photos: Pan American World Airways; right, Ewing Galloway

The Citadel rises atop a cliff in Dinant on the Meuse, with 13th century church in foreground. This resort town is noted for copper handicrafts, Montfat grottoes

The cathedral at Tournai is one of the most notable in Belgium, with Romanesque towers, a Gothic choir. Contains famous paintings by Jordaens, Massys, et

VIANDEN CASTLE IS DATED 9TH CENTURY, HAS SOME ROMAN STONES.

TINY LUXEMBOURG HAS A BIG HEART

A little smaller in size than Rhode Island, Luxembourg is varied in topography. The rugged northern section is crossed by the Ardennes. The fertile south is a country of farms, meadowland, vineyards. The city of Luxembourg, capital of the Grand Duchy, was once a walled fortress. People are most cordial.

Luxembourg

Luxembourg is a completely "different" city, with deep gorges, great bridges, and with farms right in center of tow Industries are concentrated in suburb

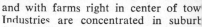

Esch-sur-Sûre is tiny town encircled by Sûre River, in the Luxembourg Ardennes.

Clervaux, situated on the Clerf Riv in the Ardennes, has 12th-century castl

Photos: Ewing Galloway; Luxer bourg National Tourist Offi

350,000 AMERICANS SEE FRANCE YEARLY

EIFFEL TOWER, TRADEMARK OF PARIS, REACHES 984 FEET INTO SKY.

he one spot that most Americans going broad head for is Paris, the city that has everything for everyone." And the hole of France is a land of enormous ariety: the quaint towns of Normandy and Brittany, the glorious sun-deck of the Riviera, the magnificent Chateau Country, winter sports in the French Alps. And everywhere, but everywhere, the food makes travelers pigs in clover.

oto: Konstantin Kostich

France PARIS

Notre Dame overlooks the bookstalls on left bank of Seine, near Place St. Michel.

Fashion show by Jacques Fath: Feminine visitors are thrilled by new "collection."

Cathedral of Notre Dame has impressive location on tiny Île de la Cité in the

Seine, the oldest part of Paris. You ca climb the tower, see great 13-ton bel

278

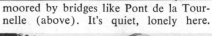

le St. Louis is next to Île de la Cité; hey're like two ships in the Seine, moored by bridges like Pont de la Tournelle (above). It's quiet, lonely here.

he Panthéon is the burial place of the atron saint of Paris, Saint Genevieve.

The Madeleine church is built like a Roman temple, with Corinthian colonnade.

Magnificent Opera House is the largest theater in the world, although it has fewer seats than the Châtelet or Milan' La Scala. Façade is lavishly decorated

Sacré-Coeur, on top of Montmartre, is oriental-looking church of white stone.

Little streets in Montmartre, full cafés, tiny shops, lead to Sacré-Coe

Photos: French Government Tourist fice; bottom left, A. L. Koolish; bott right, Pan American World Airw

Artist paints in front of tiny 12th century church of St. Julien-le-Pauvre.

Vendôme Column has bronze bas-reliefs made from cannon Napoleon captured.

Arc de Triomphe du Carrousel is reduced copy of the Arch of Septimius Severus in Rome. On top is a bronze chariot group. Building in background is the Louvre.

Bois de Boulogne is huge park on west side of Paris, with lakes and ponds, two race tracks—Auteuil and Longchamp lovely drives and fine summer restaurants

Métro is elaborate system of fourteen underground railways, with interchanges.

Les Invalides, founded as home for di abled soldiers, contains Napoleon's tom

Photos: French Gover ment Tourist Offi

The Foreign Legion parades down the tree-lined Champs-Elysées to celebrate July 14th, Bastille Day, or Fête Nationale. At top is the great *Arc de Triomphe*.

Les Halles are the great Paris produce markets, where you wind up a big night at four a.m. for a bowl of onion soup with the farmers and market workers.

The Sorbonne, the University of Paris, was started in 1253 as theological school.

Gardens of the Palais-Royal make quiet park near the fashionable shopping area.

Auteuil, in the Bois de Boulogne, has steeplechases, Longchamp has flat racing.

Kiosks for newspapers and magazines are distinctive sight along Paris boulevards

Palais du Luxembourg, once a royal residence, is noted for beautiful gardens.

Marché aux Puces, or "Flea Market," ha art, antiques, bargains for skillful buyer

Arc de Triomphe is the largest triumphal arch in the world, 160 feet high. Ride to top for magnificent view, since avenues radiate from arch in all directions.

Beautiful Sainte-Chapelle was built by St. Louis as shrine for Crown of Thorns.

The Bourse is the Paris stock exchange, housed in building like a Roman temple.

Photos: A. Milton Runyon; bottom right, French Government Tourist Office

In late afternoon the broad walks of the
Champs-Elysées fill with strollers who

keep one eye open for autos parking
the sidewalk, the other for seat at a ca

Photos: French Gove
ment   Tourist   Off

Café de Flore, on the Left Bank, has been favorite of Picasso and of Jean-Paul Sartre. Nearby are other famous places: Café du Dôme, Café des Deux Magots.

Place Pigalle is center for night life and cabarets of the more bohemian sort.

Tour d'Argent is most patrician, with pressed duck, view of Notre Dame.

France PARIS, VERSAILLES

Shops line arcaded Rue de Rivoli. Rue de Castiglione leads to Place Vendôme.

Comédie-Française does plays of Molière other greats, as well as modern drama

Folies Bergère is probably best known music hall in the world, famous for the

elaborateness of its shows, with so three hours of beauty, music and col

Photos: French Gove ment Tourist Off

Imposing western façade of great Palace of Versailles has 375 windows, many in Hall of Mirrors where World War I treaty was signed. Palace housed 10,000.

0½-mile trip to Versailles gardens is popular Sunday outing for Parisians.

Versailles fountains play on certain Sundays, are sometimes lighted at night.

France

Chartres Cathedral is noted for stained glass, sculpture, and two lofty spires, 375 ft. and 350 ft. Ornate taller one is work of gifted artist Jehan de Beuce.

Fontainebleau, second in interest only to Versailles, has lovely forest nearby.

La Malmaison was scene of literary and artistic salon of Josephine Bonaparte.

290

Étretat, 15 miles from Le Havre, is resort with beach flanked by white cliffs.

Port of Le Havre, with 2 big breakwaters, accommodates liners big as *United States*.

Honfleur, picturesque seaport at mouth of Seine, has 15th century wooden church.

Lisieux, with shrine of St. Theresa, has become an important place of pilgrimage.

Exquisite lace is made in Chartres, Le Puy, Alencon, treasured everywhere.

Vierville-sur-Mer was "Omaha Beach" of 1944 American landings in Normandy.

Mont-Saint-Michel is the great "citadel in the sea" connected with mainland by mile-long causeway. Abbey, founded in 708, is France's greatest tourist mecca

Saint-Servan (above) is part of resort area that includes Saint-Malo, Paramé.

Novelist Chateaubriand spent his boyhood in this castle near Saint-Malo

Photos: Konstantin Kostich; bottom
French Government Tourist Office

Dinan, with medieval walls, towers, is stopping place on way to Brittany coast.

Douarnenez is near tip of Brittany, picturesque fishing port for lobster, tuna.

Thatched cottages of Normandy are like their British cousins, even more homey.

Concarneau fishing boats go out into Bay of Biscay in search of sardines, tuna.

Rheims Cathedral, begun 1211, century in building, is French national symbol.

Grosse Horloge, Renaissance clock tower, is feature of Rouen, port city on Seine.

Champagne grapes, grown on Île-de-France crest, are processed at Rheims.

Hay wagons, and signs advertising *apéritif* wines, are often seen on roads.

Photos: French Government Tourist Office; bottom left, Konstantin Kostich; bottom right, Richard Joseph

Chenonceaux was the home of Diane de Poitiers, mistress of Henry II. Unique feature is bridge over Cher river, built by Delorme for Catherine de' Medici.

Chambord, the great castle of François I, stands in the midst of 13,344 acre park. The roof is remarkable for its pinnacles, sculptured chimneys, spires, and capitals.

Chaumont, with its massive feudal towers, was chateau used by Catherine de' Medici.

Church at Saint-Cyr: Balzac and Anatole France lived in this village on Loire.

Girls of Alsace still wear long plaits, and the traditional big-bowed costumes.

Strasbourg is capital of Alsace, and one of the great artistic centers of Europe.

Château de Haut-Koenigsbourg, on high Vosges peak, looks across to Germany.

Colmar, "Little Venice," is lovely town of ancient houses along the River Lauch.

Chamonix is leading summer and winter resort of the French Alps, dominated by fabulous 15,771-foot Mont Blanc. Photo shows shimmering icefield, *Mer de Glace*.

Cable railway carries skiers, tourists to great view from top of Mont Brévent.

La Clusaz is tiny winter sports resort on road between Chamonix, Annecy.

Photos: French Government Tourist Office

Biarritz, on Bay of Biscay, is one of France's most fashionable resorts. Its 7- mile beach, mild climate attracted Napoleon III, Empress Eugenie, other royalty.

Basilica at Lourdes ranks next to Rome as leading Catholic place of pilgrimage.

Thousands come annually to be cured at grotto where St. Bernadette saw vision

Photos: French Govern- ment Tourist Offic

Salies-de-Béarn, with charming homes, is health resort just east of Biarritz.

Cauterets, with its hot sulphur springs, is spa and resort of central Pyrenees.

Lake of Gaube, near Cauterets, is fine spot for hiking amid scenic splendor.

Basque game of pelote is well attended at the village of Saint-Jean-Pied-de-Port.

During Middle Ages, Saint-Jean was end of much-traveled mountain pass to Spain.

Dances of the Basque country are vigorous, colorful as the costumes of dancers.

Cannes is headquarters for the British colony on the Côte d'Azur, and yachting center for the whole Riviera, with two fine beaches, two casinos, many hotels.

St. Jean is an old fishing port at tip of lovely Cap Ferrat, abode of the wealthy.

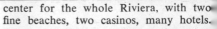

Walking is a pleasure on Cap Ferrat, fo autos are barred from many promenade:

300

Photos: Konstantin Kostich; botto left, French Government Tourist O fice; bottom right, Richard Josep

Cuisine at Nice is mixture of Parisian, Provincial and Italian—and wonderful!

Nice, Queen of the Riviera, is a major city as well as most fashionable resort.

Menton is at the very tip of the Riviera, with the Italian frontier at its edge.

Many habitués like it because the Alpes-Maritimes loom right over the beaches.

MONACO IS 370 ACRES OF GAIETY

Next to Vatican City, Monaco is th
world's smallest state. It has a popula
tion of 20,000, but only about 2,00
are actually citizens or Monégasque
They are not allowed in the Casino, bu
they don't have to pay taxes because th
Casino at Monte Carlo makes sufficier
money to finance the whole principality
Monaco has been independent ever sinc
the end of the Napoleonic Wars, in 181!

Prince's Palace is guarded, but there's
no customs barrier at Monaco frontier.

Monte Carlo Casino is world famous, not
only for its roulette wheels and other

intricate forms of gambling, but also fc
a first-class theater and concert roon

302

MUNICH IS FAMOUS FOR MARDI GRAS FESTIVITIES, COSTUME BALLS.

ROMANTIC GERMANY COMES TO NEW LIFE

West Germany, the German Federal Republic, has much to offer the tourist: its old medieval towns, gray with age, its majestic rivers and idyllic landscapes. While the people are throwing much of their energy into reconstruction, they have time for fun, and Germany now has some of the gayest night life in Europe. Frankfurt is good place for first stop.

Pension Anton Lang at Oberammergau:
Passion Play is performed every 10 years.

Oberammergau Play is now presented in
modern theater, needs 1250 performers.

Between Passion Plays, the residents of
Oberammergau carve religious figures.

Garmisch-Partenkirchen, site of Olympic
winter games in 1936, is great ski resort

Photos: A. L. Koolish; center left
and Danube River, German Tourist Information Office; bottom
left, TWA Trans World Airline

Ehrenfels Castle is 13th century relic, amid terraced vineyards on Rhine river.

Danube River at Riedlingen (below): After the Volga, it's continent's longest.

Lindau is old town on an island in Lake Constance, with bridges to mainland.

Kehlsteinhaus at Berchtesgaden looks out over the beautiful Salzburg Alps.

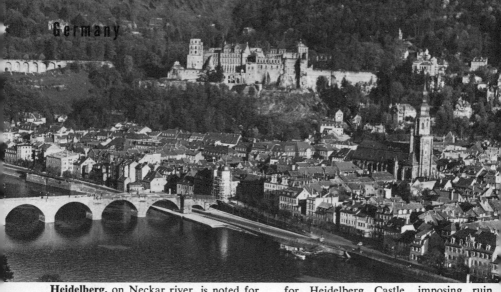

Heidelberg, on Neckar river, is noted for country's most famous university, and for Heidelberg Castle, imposing ruin built and rebuilt over past 700 years.

Mainz, one of Germany's great historical cities, celebrates Rose Monday Festival.

The Black Forest has modest ski lodges, plush resort centers like Baden-Baden.

"Trinkhalle" at **Baden-Baden** is lovely spot to imbibe healthful spring waters.

Photos: German Tourist Information Office

Cologne at night: majestic cathedral sustained only slight damage in the war.

Begun in 1248, it was completed in 1880; contains relics of Wise Men of the East.

Berlin's main street, Kurfürstendamm, is again busy with shopping, entertainment.

This is view of the restored boulevard as it looks from the Kempinski Hotel.

AUSTRIA IS LAND OF ALPS, GREEN VALLEYS, AND MUSIC

Austria, the "heart of Europe," is famed for its towering Alps, its meadows and forests and villages, and its wealth of entertainment, climaxed by the Salzburg Music Festival. You'll enjoy seeing the gay Tyrolean costumes, flowered shawls and dirndls. You'll wander in fairy-tale villages like this one in the Tyrol.

Kitzbühel is a Tyrolean medieval town that is both winter and summer resort.

Innsbruck's Maria Theresa Street leads toward high peaks of the Eastern Alps.

Photos: Austrian State Tourist Department; top, Konstantin Kostich

The Graben, the "moat," is now principal shopping street in great city of Vienna.

Belvedere Palace was built for Prince Eugene who kept the Turks out of Europe.

Vienna's Opera House, one of world's renowned, is only one at street level.

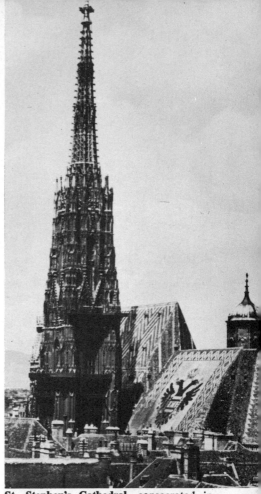

St. Stephen's Cathedral, consecrated in 1147, has slender 448-foot Gothic spire.

The famous "white horses of Vienna" give performance at Salzburg Festival.

Austria

How to climb an ice wall is taught at the High Alpine School at Heiligenblut.

Church at St. Wolfgang contains Pacher altar, world's most valuable wood carving.

Zell am See, because of conjunction of air currents, is ideal place for gliding.

At Salzburg Festival, Hofmannsthal's "Jedermann" is staged on the domplatz.

Peasant festival at Schwaz: This is a typical feature of the Austrian scene.

Photos: Austrian State Tourist Department; bottom left, Pan American World Airways

SWITZERLAND MEANS MOUNTAINS AND WATCHES AND CHOCOLATES

JUNGFRAU'S MIGHTY 13,650-FT. PEAK WAS FIRST CLIMBED IN 1811.

In winter, Switzerland is unquestionably the winter sports capital of the world, and the glistening snow brings bright new beauty to its tremendous mountains. In summer, the sparkling lake resorts are at their best. Throughout the year, the country is one of boundless hospitality with some of the best food and the most comfortable hotels in the world. If you like creature comforts, this is for you!

Photo: A. L. Koolish

Switzerland

League of Nations buildings at Geneva symbolize Switzerland as great neutral.

This is a typical holiday home in Swiss chalet style, at Villars-sur-Ollon, Vaud.

Calvin Memorial in Geneva's *Promenade des Bastions* hails freedom of religion.

The Lake of Geneva is enlivened by many trim excursion steamers which take you from Geneva, at west end of lake, to Lausanne, Vevey, Montreux, other points.

Photos: Swiss National Travel Office; top right, TWA Trans World Airline

Castle of Chillon, near Montreux on Lake Geneva, is one of the best preserved medieval castles in Europe—the scene of Byron's poem, "The Prisoner of Chillon."

Montreux itself is a charming town, huddled between the lake and the Alpine peak of Rochers de Naye, 6,700 feet. This is chief resort area of French Switzerland.

Photos: TWA Trans World Airline; bottom, Konstantin Kostich

Switzerland

Open air train takes passengers up the scenic slopes of Rigi, near Lucerne.

Lucerne is gateway to "Land of William Tell." This is Hofkirche, founded in 735

Older parts of Lucerne, with charming houses like this, are on right bank of

the Reuss. Vacation capital of Switze land, Lucerne has magnificent scener

Lake steamer approaching Lucerne on west shore of the lake. Lake Lucerne is one of the most beautiful in Europe, with its charming irregularity, lovely views.

One of the most characteristic features of Lucerne is the Kapell-Brücke, roofed bridge crossing the river diagonally. It contains 112 paintings of local history.

Photos: Charles Marschalek

Switzerland

St. Moritz is summer and winter sports center, often scene of winter Olympics.

At Jungfraujoch you may ride sledge drawn by Polar huskies across glacier

Interlaken, between the lakes of Thun and Brienz, is one of the oldest and most popular of Swiss resorts, with it superb view of the Jungfrau to the south

Photos: Swiss National Travel Of fice; bottom, Charles Marschale

View from Jungfraujoch is magnificent. This is the highest point in Europe that is reached by rail—over 11,000 feet. Innumerable summits are seen all around.

Outdoor shopping in Lugano: this ancient town in the south is Italian in character.

Lido Beach at Lugano offers fine food, amidst gorgeous lake and mountain views.

Photos: A. L. Koolish; bottom, Swiss National Travel Office

The noble Grossmünster church and the Helmhaus museum are cherished land- marks of Zurich, largest city in Switzer land, on Lake of Zurich, Limmat river

Basel, at French and German borders on Rhine, has market that's open every day.

Basel's new Industries Fair Building ha giant clock with 12-ft. sweep second han

Photos: Swiss National Travel Off

Houses of Parliament in Berne, capital of Switzerland. With its arcades on the older streets, and its many fountains, Berne's medieval air attracts visitors.

Visitors to library of St. Gall's Abbey put on slippers to protect ancient floors.

Clock Tower is Berne's traditional landmark and the bear is the city's mascot.

Switzerland

Davos, in 5,000-foot high valley, is first-rank place for skating and skiing.

Sports train of Gornergrat railway at Zermatt climbs toward the Matterhorn.

Cresta Toboggan Run, at St. Moritz, is ¾ mile long, with a drop of 500 feet.

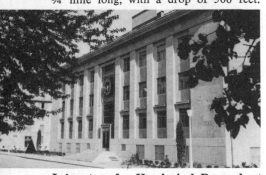

Laboratory for Horological Research at Neuchâtel is pride of the watch industry.

Travelers in Zurich candy shop stock u on the world-famous Swiss chocolate

Photos: Swiss National Travel Offi

Voyage 8
THE MEDITERRANEAN

TWA Constellation gets to Rome fast.

Most people are anxious to visit the "cradle of Western civilization" that the Mediterranean area represents, with such seats of early culture and religious development as Rome, Athens, Venice, Jerusalem and other ancient cities.

There are many pleasant ways to get to the Mediterranean. Four of the major airlines fly directly to Rome from New York: TWA, Air France, Pan American, and LAI, the Italian airline. And of course Rome is one of the major terminals of lines from northern Europe, British European, Scandinavian, KLM, Swissair. And air connections are good for other points, Portugal, Spain, Greece, Israel and all around the 2,400 mile length of the Mediterranean Sea.

By ship, there are also splendid possibilities. Two of the finest of American ships are the *Independence* and *Constitution* of the American Export Lines. They call at Gibraltar, Cannes and Genoa on way to Naples. And the same line has four

smaller ships, *Excalibur, Excambion, Exeter* and *Exochorda,* which circle around the Mediterranean, calling at a number of ports. Italian Line ships include *Saturnia, Vulcania* and luxurious new *Cristoforo Colombo.* A number of other services offer variety for different tastes and purses.

However you go, you'll find the Mediterranean area warm and sunny. The climate has become so famous that other regions around the world often advertise their "Mediterranean-like climate." And you are always surrounded by history: from the days of the Phoenicians, through glories of Carthage, Greece and Rome, down to present day importance as great shipping lane between ports of Europe, Asia.

Gibraltar is seen from "Independence."

Photos: TWA Trans World Airline; bottom, American Export Lines

PORTUGAL INVITES YOU
TO ITS SUNNY COAST

Portugal offers much charm for visitors who want to get off beaten pathways. Its principal cities have modern hotels and there are "tourist inns" in the smaller places. Main playland of the country is along the coast, the Portuguese Riviera, with resorts like Estoril and Cascais. Lisbon is one of the great international capitals of the world, with a "different" atmosphere that stems from its glamorous past when Portugal ruled half the New World. Monument above is in memory of the Marques de Pombal who rebuilt Lisbon after the 1755 earthquake.

Portugal

Rossio Square is geographical center of Lisbon. It has flower market, statue of Peter the 4th, and is flanked by national theater and the central railroad station

Castle of St. George was site of famous battle that repulsed the Moors in 1147.

Alfama district, crowded and colorful is clustered about 12th century cathedral

Sintra, 14 miles northwest of Lisbon, has the Palace of Pena perched high on a hill above the town, most fascinating of the country's magnificent old royal palaces.

Fishing is major occupation in the many harbors of Portugal. These gaily painted boats are at Lisbon. Some fishermen use nets that are floated out from the shore.

Photos: TWA Trans World Airline

Basilica of Shrine of Our Lady at Fátima attracts almost as many as Lourdes.

Coimbra is Portugal's university city. "S Velha" is a 12th century Roman edifice

Estoril is fabulous seaside resort, just 15 miles from Lisbon, with magnificent

beach, flower gardens, casino, fine hotel bridle paths by the sea and up into hill

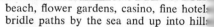

Oporto, second city of Portugal, is famous for port wine. This is cathedral.

Nazaré is typical fishing village wher men wear bright plaids and stocking cap

Photos: Casa de Portugal; top lef
center, TWA Trans World Airlin

Madeira, Portuguese island 625 miles to southwest of Lisbon, is known as "Pearl of the Atlantic." S.S. *Independence* is shown in beautiful harbor of Funchal.

Wood-sled transportation indicates the primitiveness of life on Madeira island.

Santa Maria is one of the 9 main Azores islands, 1200 miles to west of Lisbon.

Photos: Deane Dickason (Ewing Galloway);
bottom left, Burton Holmes (Ewing Galloway);
bottom right, TWA Trans World Airline.

SPAIN IS LAND OF GREAT TRADITIONS

Spanish civilization dates back to the stone age. The Basques may be descended from Cro-Magnon man whose art has been found in caves at Altamira. The history of Spain is long and involved, but it reached a great climax after Columbus' discovery of America sparked enormous expansion of the empire which came to include almost all of the Americas and around the world to the Philippines. The Spain of today is a land of color, music and gaiety, with many reminders of past glories. Madrid (Plaza Mayor above) is Spain's capital and geographical center.

Photo: Spanish State Tourist Office

Castellana Hilton Hotel is newest and most luxurious in the gay city of Madrid.

Madrid's newer sections with spacious streets contrast with the old quarters.

With over a million population, Madrid has subway, other modern transportation.

Calle de Alcalá is one of several wide tree-lined boulevards in modern Madrid.

Prado Museum is one of world's greatest, with works of Velázquez, other masters.

Even in busy Madrid, one can see farm carts lumbering slowly along to market.

Puerta del Sol, once one of gates of old ramparts of Madrid leveled 4 centuries ago, has undergone a recent face-lifting and become principal square of the city.

Throne Room is one of many impressive parlors in the sumptuous Royal Palace.

Palace, built on the site of old alcazar houses many of Spain's treasures of art

Photos: Spanish State Tourist Office; top left, TWA Trans World Airline; top right, Charles Marschale

Outstanding feature of Madrid is the great number of broad squares and noble avenues. Here the horses of the Cibeles Fountain head for the Calle de Alcalá.

Rose gardens are a feature of beautiful Retiro Park, with its lovely trees, lake.

Concert at Retiro Park is at other end of entertainment scale from 2 bull rings.

Photos: Spanish State Tourist Office

San Juan de los Reyes, in Toledo, was built by Ferdinand and Isabella.

Santo Tomé church houses the painting by El Greco, *The Burial of Count Orgaz.*

Toledo's greatest glory is its splendid cathedral, a combination of five styles.

Steep cobbled streets of Toledo remind one of Moorish towns of North Africa.

Photos: TWA Trans World Airline; bottom right, Richard Joseph

Imposing walls of Toledo include the Bisagra Gate (above) and the Mudejar Gate. Most noteworthy secular building is the alcazar, palace of King Charles V.

Many-turreted alcazar, in Segovia, was site of crowning of Queen Isabella I.

Lofty Roman aqueduct, with 170 arches, is still used to supply water to Segovia.

Photos: TWA Trans World Airline; bottom, Richard Joseph

Granada's Alhambra, home of Moorish kings, is the finest Moorish art in Spain.

Grapes, for home use, and olives for export, are Spain's main industrial crops.

Granada gypsies perform a gay dance for tourists before one of their houses.

Málaga, noted for sweet Malaga wine, is famed winter resort on the Mediterranean.

It is one of the oldest cities of Spain, said to have been founded by Phoenicians.

Spain

Salon Arabe shows exquisite decorations of the alcazar, Moorish palace in Seville.

Lofty Giralda Tower, over 300 feet high, is part of beautiful cathedral of Seville.

Some of Spain's farming is still done by camel-power, as for many centuries past.

Spanish mantillas come into their own at the Seville Fair which follows Holy Week.

Photos: Spanish State Tourist Office; top right, Pan American World Airways

335

Spain

Costa Brava (rugged coast) is section between the French Riviera and Barcelona.

Fight over design prevented completion of Barcelona's Church of the Holy Family.

Battle-scarred gates lead to Valencia, Spain's third city, near Mediterranean.

Spain is noted for its many fiestas at different seasons, this one at Santander.

Bullfight at El Espinar, near Barcelona, (below) is one of 500 a year in Spain.

Santander is surrounded by the Picos de Europa, mountains that rise to 8800 feet.

Santiago de Compostela, at Spain's northwest tip, is a pilgrim city of world renown.

Spain

Country homes in Majorca feature cosy chimney corner seats by the kitchen fire.

Mountain village of Valldemosa is on the Spanish island of Majorca, in Balearics.

Canary Islands are Spanish possessions off northwest Africa. This is Santa Cruz.

Old houses at Sóller, on Majorca, are reflected in waters on the picturesque harbor. The town is surrounded by orange trees; its port ships oranges and wine.

TUNISIA IS SITE OF ANCIENT CARTHAGE

700,000 people lived in Carthage before the time of Christ; now it's a desolate plain. When you visit Tunisia, in North Africa, you'll feel that ancient history peers over your 20th century shoulder.

Old Moslem quarter of Tunis is a maze of crooked streets, extensive bazaars.

Tunis is capital of Tunisia and a mecca for tourists looking for the unusual.

In the tree-lined square which runs from cathedral to port are many sidewalk cafés.

Newly excavated ruins of Carthage baths bring back memories of high school Latin.

Photos: TWA Trans World Airline

ALGERIA IS FRANCE IN AFRICA

Whereas Tunisia and Morocco are Protectorates, Algeria has a much closer link, being an actual Department. In Algiers, the capital, you might imagine that you were in slower-moving version of Paris.

Algiers is chief Mediterranean port of French North Africa. It stretches along the bay for ten miles, its white houses gleaming brilliantly in the strong sun.

Famous "Ouled-Naïl" dancers perform at tiny Bou-Saâda, 125 miles from Algiers.

Dancers take their name from Ouled-Naï mountains, on edge of the Sahara desert

Photos: TWA Trans World Air line; bottom, Richard Josep

Cathedral on Place Malakoff is one of the many impressive buildings in Algiers.

Hammam-Meskoutine is noted spa with hot springs in the Constantine mountains.

Rommel Gorge from above: Atlas mountains cut off desert interior from the sea.

Casbah section of old Algiers has real labyrinth of narrow terraced streets.

Roman ruins at Djemila include arch of triumph, a forum, 3rd century temple.

ANCIENT, MODERN MIX IN MOROCCO

Morocco extends along the Atlantic and Mediterranean at northwest corner of Africa. It's divided into French Morocco, Spanish Morocco, and the International Zone of Tangier, across from Gibraltar.

Casablanca, the largest city of French Morocco, was scene of history-making conference between President Roosevelt and Prime Minister Churchill in 1943.

Modern-looking Anfa Hotel, on a green bluff outside the city, was meeting site.

Modern Casablanca forms a semicircle around old city. This is the Post Office.

342

THE COLOSSEUM IS BEST KNOWN SYMBOL OF MIGHT OF ANCIENT ROME.

SUNNY ITALY IS A PARADISE ON EARTH

The surrounding sea and the protecting Alps give Italy a wonderfully balanced climate in both winter and summer. The scenery has great variety: lovely beaches, beautiful lake resorts, magnificent Alps and Apennines and Dolomites. Lovers of culture, history find incomparable wealth in Italian art and archeology.

Photo: TWA Trans World Airline

The Colosseum had room for 50,000. Cross commemorates the early Christian martyrs who died in the amphitheater victims of lions, sport of early Romans

Forum Romanum was the center of economic, political and religious life of
ancient Rome. This is site of Castor's
Temple and temple of the vestal virgins.

The Tiber River winds through Rome much as the Seine through Paris, the Thames through London. This is Sant' Angelo bridge, with dome of St. Peter's.

Vatican Library is one of world's most beautiful. Contains over half a million books, and many rare manuscripts like 4th century Codex Vaticanus of Bible.

Photos: Konstantin Kostich; bottom, Italian State Tourist Office

St. Peter's, covering an area of 163,728 square feet, is largest, most majestic of Christian churches. Built by Emperor Constantine, dome is by Michelangelo.

Papal Fountain has insignia of the Chigi, same shape as crown worn by Pope Pius.

Swiss Guards have served at the Holy See as attendants of the Pope since 1505.

Photos: TWA Trans World Airline; bottom left, Copyright, Herbert List (Magnum); bottom right, Italian State Tourist Office

The Spanish Steps, 137 of them, cascade down the slope of Pincian Hill, joining

Church of Santa Trinità dei Monti with Piazza di Spagna and Via Condotti below.

Hotel Hassler, near top of Spanish Steps, has roof garden restaurant with a view.

Motorists in Rome honor ancient custom by giving police special Epiphany gifts.

Photos: TWA Trans World Airline; bottom left, A. Milton Runyon; bottom right, Pan American World Airways

From this balcony on the Piazza Venezia,
Benito Mussolini often addressed throngs.

Casina Valadier is delightful restaurant
on Pincian Hill, overlooking all Rome.

Monument to Victor Emmanuel II is
Bréscia marble structure of great size.

The work of Giuseppe Sacconi, it celebrates the realization of Italian unity.

Photos: A. Milton Runyon; bottom, TWA Trans World Airline

Castel Sant'Angelo, approached by the celebrated Sant'Angelo bridge over the Tiber, was built at command of Emperor Hadrian as mausoleum for Roman rulers.

Formal gardens of Castel Gandolfo: This is country residence of the Pope, south of Rome on the Appian Way, and by the Lateran treaty now part of Vatican City.

Photos: TWA Trans World Airline; bottom, Konstantin Kostich

Claudian Aqueduct, with its series of superb arches, was built in year 52 A.D.

Villa d'Este, with fountains, terraced gardens, is beauty spot at nearby Tivoli.

Appian Way is the old highway to Rome from the south, lined with cypress trees.

Tivoli, viewed from Villa d'Este: town is noted for waterfalls, Hadrian's villa.

Photos: Konstantin Kostich; top left, TWA Trans World Airline

Florence was "cradle of the Italian Renaissance." Uffizi Palace, in background, has one of world's richest collections of paintings and 1,500,000 volume library

Photo: Konstantin Kostich

Ponte Vecchio, across the Arno, contains many tiny shops. Gallery across top, that connected Uffizi Palace (tower at left) with Pitti Palace, was partly destroyed.

Beautiful Boboli gardens are on grounds of Pitti Palace, once residence of the great Medici family, Florentine statesmen, rulers, and patrons of the arts.

Photos: TWA Trans World Airline; bottom, Italian State Tourist Office

Italy VENICE

The mystic quality of Venice expresses itself in this photo of gondolas before San Marco square, with Santa Maria della Salute seen through early evening haze

Venice is intricate network of canals, big and small, with countless bridges.

Bridge of Sighs was passage for prisoners from Ducal Palace to airless cell

354

Photos: A. Milton Runyon
bottom left, Richard Josep

Rialto Bridge over the Grand Canal has two rows of shops, twelve on each side.

Ca' d'Oro, the Golden House, is splendid home of 15th century Venetian patriarch.

Cathedral of San Marco, dedicated in 830 to patron saint of Venice, is most ornate.

Grand Canal, 2 miles long, is the chief artery of Venice, winding in an S-curve from the Piazza San Marco to the railroad station. Width averages 228 feet.

Italy

From island in harbor one looks across to San Marco square with its 325-foot Campanile and magnificent Palace of the Doges who ruled Venice in days of glory.

Traffic on canals requires signal light; gondoliers shout at narrow intersections.

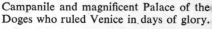

Floating vegetable market: motorboat are now offering competition to gondolas

356

Photos: Konstantin Kostich; bottom left, Richard Joseph; bottom right, Italian State Tourist Office

Chioggia, 15 miles south of Venice, is one of Italy's major fishing centers, known for picturesqueness of its sails. Venice defeated Genoa in battles here.

Ponte Scaligero is one of ten bridges across the Adige at Verona. Strife between two powerful families of Verona was symbolized in *Romeo and Juliet*.

At top of cable railway at Ortisei, you can have refreshments while enjoying the magnificent panorama. Town is known for carving of toys, religious articles.

Wild flowers add to beauty of Dolomites near principal resort, Cortina d'Ampezzo.

Dolomite Alps of northern Italy are known for vivid sunrise, sunset colors.

In driving through Dolomites, you often come on wayside shrines on roads that reach almost 9,000 feet. Highest peak is Marmolada, towering up 10,964 feet.

Cortina d'Ampezzo is both a summer and winter resort, in center of Dolomites, one of Europe's finest mountain areas. Brenner Pass is 45 miles to northwest.

Photo: Konstantin Kostich; bottom, Italian State Tourist Office

Milan cathedral is elaborately decorated with over 100 pinnacles, 3,000 statues.

An elevator takes you to the roof where you can see white marble figures close by.

Opposite Milan cathedral is the Galleria Vittorio Emanuele where all Milan meets.

Castello Sforzesco was once a barracks, now interesting archeological museum.

Milan, chief industrial center of Italy, has world's grandest railroad station.

Convent with Leonardo's *Last Supper* is next to Santa Maria delle Grazie church.

La Scala Opera House, with its red and gold auditorium, is world's most noted.

Leonardo da Vinci—painter, sculptor, architect and engineer—faces La Scala.

Bellagio is on tip of promontory that divides beautiful Lake Como into its two southern arms. This popular resort has many villas, gardens, ancient church.

Lake Como, Italy's 3rd largest, is in Lombardy, 25 miles to north of Milan.

Lake steamers call at resorts of Como Bellagio, Lecco, Tremezzo, and others

Photos: Italian State Tourist Office; bottom, Konstantin Kostic

Lake Garda has wonderfully clear blue waters, many lovely white villages. This is Riva, at northwest extremity of the lake, with palace built by the Venetians.

Lake Maggiore contains famous Borromean Islands. This is view from Isola Bella, site of 1934 conference at which Germany denounced the Versailles treaty.

Photos: Konstantin Kostich; bottom, Charles Marschalek

Genoa, port city at center of the Italian Riviera, rises from waterfront to height of over 1,000 feet in surrounding hills. Municipal palace has letters of Columbus.

Maritime Station at Genoa is home port of Italian Line ships and port of call of many others. Genoa rivals Marseilles as chief seaport of the Mediterranean.

Photos: Konstantin Kostich; bottom, Italian State Tourist Office

Italy

Cathedral at Orvieto is noted for its gleaming façade, miracle of fine carving.

The 12th century church of St. Francis of Assisi is monument to his gentle spirit.

Pisa's graceful Leaning Tower is 180 ft. high, and 14 ft. out of perpendicular.

Lerici is resort on Gulf of Spezia, one of largest, safest Mediterranean harbors.

Nearby is a 12th century Pisan castle, which is now used as marine observatory.

Photos: Konstantin Kostich; center left, Italian State Tourist Office

Greatest spectacle in Naples is lovely view across the bay to no-longer-smoking Vesuvius. Many parts of the city have grown up into the surrounding hills and are reached by funiculars. Neapolitans are famous for songs like *Santa Lucia*

Photo: TWA Trans World Airline

Caruso was hissed at his debut at San Carlo Opera House. Though he was often urged to return after he made his fame international, he would never come back.

Castel dell'Ovo (Castle of the Egg) is on its own tiny island opposite the Via Parthenope where the principal hotels of Naples are located. The medieval castle was begun by the Norman King William I, completed and modified by his successors.

Umberto I Square is the center of lovely Capri.

Marina Piccola looks out to great Faraglioni rocks.

Visitors arrive at Capri by small steamers from Naples, a distance of 20 miles.

Blue Grotto gets its name from dazzling blue light produced by the bright sun.

Funicular railway links Marina Grande with town of Capri, 456 feet higher up.

Photos: TWA Trans World Airline

Pompeii was buried by the eruption of Vesuvius in 79 A.D. This is the Forum.

Temple of Apollo is one of ruins found by excavations that were begun in 1763.

Lava-paved streets of Pompeii were used by chariots of city's 20,000 residents.

Well-preserved homes are chief source of information about ancient domestic life.

Sorrento is charmingly situated amid orange and lemon groves on mountainous peninsula south of Bay of Naples. *Come Back to Sorrento* is more than a song.

Most dramatic road in Italy is the one from Sorrento to Amalfi, along rugged coast and over the hills that rise to a 4,734 foot height in Monte Sant'Angelo.

Photos: Konstantin Kostich

Amalfi was great seaport in 11th century, rivaling Naples and Venice. Today it's perfect spot for enjoying the southwest coast. Amalfi Drive is a scenic wonder.

Paestum, whose roots go back to the 6th century B.C., was not destroyed by cataclysm as was Pompeii. After fall of the Empire, malaria drove inhabitants away.

Photos: Konstantin Kostich

Positano, 6 miles west of Amalfi, is one of the most beautiful unspoiled fishing villages where one can live like a king on even Social Security rate of income.

Fishermen now land on Salerno beaches where Allied landing forces fought bitterly against the Germans during fierce battle of September 9th to 16th, 1943.

Photos: Konstantin Kostich

373

Sicily is known as "Island of the Sun" and brightness penetrates narrow alleys.

From Taormina, you can see Sicily's Mt. Etna, highest active volcano in Europe.

Greek Theater of Syracuse is largest, most beautiful of all the Hellenic ruins.

Palermo at night: With over 500,000 inhabitants, it is one of Italy's largest and most aristocratic cities. Buildings range from Norman-Arab to 20th century.

TEMPLE OF JUPITER DATES FROM DAYS OF ROMAN RULE IN ATHENS.

THE MAJESTY OF GREECE LIVES ON

Whether or not you have read Socrates, Plato and Aristotle, you want to know something of the great civilization that reached its peak more than four centuries before Christ. A visit to the Acropolis time-machines you back through the centuries. And you'll find modern Athens a bright and busy city of 1¼ million.

Academy of Athens, University of Athens and National Library are proud buildings of modern Athens. The city is political, economic and cultural center of Greece.

Your imagination can place thousands of listeners in the vast Temple of Music.

Palace guard reminds you that in 1946 a plebiscite called for return of monarch.

Photos: Royal Greek Embassy Information Service; bottom left, S. A. Booth; bottom right, Richard Joseph

The Acropolis rises proudly on 180-foot hill above the Attic plain. The Parthenon and many large buildings were built in Golden Age of Pericles, 2400 years ago.

Picturesque Corfu, second largest of the Ionian islands, was Homer's "Scheria."

The Caryatids have carried Erechtheum roof on their heads about 24 centuries.

YUGOSLAVIA OFFERS SCENIC ADVENTURE

Yugoslavia is now a member of European Travel Commission and is inviting tourists to enjoy its good food and superb scenery of places like Dubrovnik and the Dalmatian Island of Rab in the Adriatic.

Parliament in Belgrade: Strategic site of capital makes it "key to Balkans."

Budva is port city on Adriatic, with an Orthodox Eastern cathedral, built 1418.

Dubrovnik, walled city on south coast, was called Arragosa, the root of *argosy*.

Jajce is medieval town on Vrbas river, with ruined castle and lovely waterfall.

Dome of Rock mosque is on site of temple where Jesus turned out money changers.

PAST AND PRESENT MEET IN ISRAEL

Modern Israel has much to offer visitors who are politically and socially aware of the ferment of our times. And as the ancient "Land of the Bible" it attracts pilgrims to Jerusalem, the River Jordan, Nazareth, Tiberias on the Sea of Galilee, and Mount Zion. New roads, hotels make it easy to visit old and new Israel.

Israel

Sunset over Jerusalem: View shows the great no man's land between the old city and the new. On left is King David hotel. Buildings at right are in Arab sector.

Haifa, seen from Mt. Carmel, is principal seaport of Israel and industrial center.

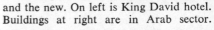

The Sea of Galilee is associated with many events of New Testament history.

Photos: Robert Capa (Magnum); bottom, Israel National Tourist Center

Typical of modern architecture of Israel is YMCA building near Jerusalem's walls.

Street vendor's shop looks archaic, but he has modern convenience of telephone.

From Mount of Olives you see whole of Jerusalem spread out before you, and much of it seems as it might have been 2000 years ago, behind the ancient wall.

The carpenter shop at Nazareth is place that attracts many pilgrims to Israel.

Tel Aviv from the air: Largest city and commercial hub, with 300,000 population.

SIRKECI SQUARE IN ISTANBUL IS THE BUSY CENTER OF A BUSY CITY.

TURKEY IS LINK
BETWEEN EAST, WEST

Mention of Istanbul or the Golden Horn probably puts you in mind of a thriller by Eric Ambler or a movie of Humphrey Bogart's. Turkey is an ancient land that used to join Europe, Africa and Asia in its empire. Istanbul, once Constantinople, is partly in Europe, partly Asia. It is terminus of famous Orient Express.

Photo: Turkish Information Office

Ankara is centrally located modern city, now the fast-growing capital of Turkey.

These old Roman ruins are near Smyrna, port long known for its export of figs.

Bosporus Strait connects the Sea of Marmara and the Black Sea, separating European and Asian Turkey. The tower is part of Rumeli Hisar fortifications.

From dock near the Yeni (New) Mosque, ferry boats leave for Bosporus crossing.

International commuters read the news on daily trip between Europe and Asia.

Photos: Turkish Information Office

BEIRUT, MAIN PORT FOR LEVANT STATES, IS CAPITAL OF LEBANON.

LEBANON HAS ANCIENT LURE

Lebanon is a tiny country, just 120 miles long and 35 wide, proclaimed an independent nation in 1941. Beirut, the capital, was a flourishing Phoenician city some 3000 years ago. Today it is trade and transportation center for both Oriental and Western Worlds, the gateway for travelers to Jordan and to Israel.

Photo: Deane Dickason (Ewing Galloway)

Voyage 9
ROUND-THE-WORLD CRUISE

"President Cleveland" at Hong Kong.

Pan American "Clipper" in Hawaii.

A Round-the-World Cruise is the most glamorous of voyages: it is the sort of trip that's offered as the grand prize in a contest, the kind that wealthy travelers with plenty of time take aboard a luxury liner like the *Caronia,* or that more and more people are now making by air, or a combination of air and sea. Each year a few lucky souls embark on conducted tours around the world, taking about 3 months, and costing some $5,000 and up apiece.

On the less expensive side, you can go all the way around the world on the American President liners, *President Polk* and *President Monroe,* in about 14 weeks, at fares as low as $2,000 each. There are special sightseeing arrangements in most ports. By air, Pan American

routes that cover 83 countries and colonies make it possible to plan an itinerary that will reach your interests in almost any part of the globe. And all sorts of ship-and-air combinations are possible: by way of Pan American, TWA, Northwest Orient Airlines, and such ship lines as American Export, Matson Line, American President, and the several British lines that cover points in India and Africa.

Should South Africa be interesting to you, Farrell Line ships will take you directly to Capetown. And for a quick return, Pan American has through-plane service.

Most round-the-world itineraries start westward and make Hawaii the first port of call—and it's such a glamorous one you may decide to put in all your vacation time there!

Photos: American President Lines and Pan American World Airways

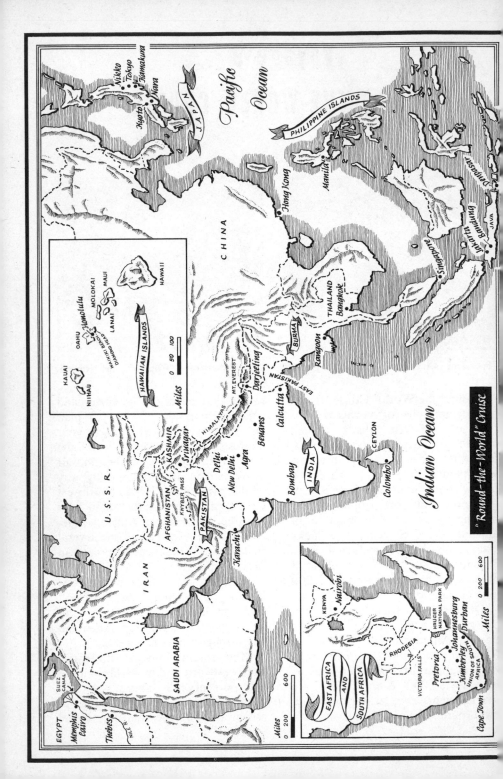

"Round-the-World" Cruise

MILD CLIMATE, LOVELY BEACHES MAKE HAWAII TRUE GARDEN SPOT.

HAWAII IS OUR TROPICAL PARADISE

Ever since Captain Cook discovered the Hawaiian Islands in 1778, their magic has been known to the world—a land of mild climate the year round (the mean annual temperature is about 75°), of fine white sand beaches, of subtropical ocean waters, and of smiling, friendly natives. It's 10 hours by air from West Coast.

Photo: Hawaii Visitors Bureau

Hawaii

The bi-annual transpacific yacht races are alternated with the local invitation series.

Fishing with thrownet is real art; needs sharp eye, quick coördination.

At famous Waikiki Beach, Honolulu, vacationists may go for exciting rides in outrigger canoes and double-hulle catamarans. Diamond Head is at the lef•

Luxurious Royal Hawaiian Hotel is right at the edge of Waikiki beach, and so is the friendly Moana. At right is the Outrigger Club, for surf boards and canoes.

Little island youngster, clad in bright Aloha shirt, makes friends with visitor.

During Aloha festival, Hawaiian enacts old ways, pounding poi in the old style.

A half-hour's drive from Honolulu's center, across famous Nuuanu Pali, brings you to beach area on windward side of Oahu, a splendid place for surf fishing

Waimea Canyon, on the island of Kauai, is the "Grand Canyon" of Hawaii, cutting through the verdure of the lush, green island with gorges similar to Colorado's

You won't be able to match the skill of these surfboard riders at first try, but the simpler styles are not hard to learn. First successful ride is a great thrill.

The Blow Hole, on Koko Head, is a salt water geyser, caused by rush of the tide.

Ala Moana yacht harbor, at entrance to Ala Wai canal, has boats from afar.

Hawaii

S.S. Lurline passes Diamond Head. Voyage from California is a delightful one.

Girls with bare brown shoulders, flower leis, perform the symbolic Hawaiian hula.

At Kauai island, natives gather round the shores of Nawiliwili bay for a "hukilau" during which they pull in huge nets from the indigo-colored sea, loaded with fish.

Photos: Hawaii Visitors Bureau; top left, Matson Lines

NEARLY 50,000 CLIMB PERFECT CONE OF FUJIYAMA EVERY SUMMER.

JAPAN IS LAND OF EXQUISITE BEAUTY

The four islands of Japan offer scenery of every conceivable type: forests, lakes, mountains, swift rivers, hot springs, and miles of rice paddies. The charming gardens feature foliage rather than blooms. The cities offer Western comforts, but are filled with gaudy color. Buddhist temples, Shinto shrines are everywhere.

Tokyo, capital of Japan, is on the shore of the Bay of Tokyo; it is traversed by several streams. In upper left, surrounded by moat, is Imperial Palace and grounds.

Ginza Street, brilliantly lit at night, is Tokyo's fashionable shopping district.

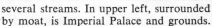

Diet Building is Tokyo's impressive legislative headquarters, on high hill.

Photos: Japan Travel Bureau; bottom left, Ewing Galloway; bottom right, I. R. Lorwin (Ewing Galloway)

Hachiman Shinto Shrine, at Kamakura, was built 1063, features long stairway.

Kamakura is beach resort on Sagami Bay, about an hour from Tokyo by train, car.

Great bronze Buddha of Kamakura stands 42 ft. high and dates from the year 1252.

The Kabuki-za in Tokyo is the best-known theater where classical drama is done.

Japan KYOTO, NARA, NIKKO

Stepping stones in Heian Shrine's garden are set crooked, so devils will fall off.

Sanju-Sangen-do Hall, Kyoto, has 1,001 statues of Kannon, the Goddess of Mercy.

Kyoto has some 3,000 Buddhist temples and Shinto shrines. One of most beautiful is Heian shrine, originally built in 794. This is one of Kyoto's several festivals.

396

Photos: Ewing Galloway; Three Lions; Japan Travel Bureau

Nikko, about 90 miles north of Tokyo, is summer resort in the Japanese Alps. It has 141,000-acre Nikko National Park. This is Shinto ceremony at Ieyasu Tomb.

New Year's Day: On this national holiday geisha girls play battledore, shuttlecock.

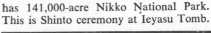

Nara's great 13-foot bell is in world's largest wooden building, Daibutsu-Den.

HONG KONG IS BUSIEST PORT OF FAR EAST

Typical of the British Crown Colony of Hong Kong are streets so steep that they have to be terraced into steps. 28,000 British soldiers guard 2 million people.

From top of Victoria Peak you get view of tall buildings of Hong Kong and its harbor beyond. The cable railway trip up 1800-foot peak is a tourist favorite.

White pagoda is on estate of Aw Boon Haw, fabulous owner of "Tiger Balm."

Fishing junks tie up at port of Aberdeen, on either side of island from Hong Kong.

Photos: Pan American World Airways

Hong Kong is one of the world's few free ports, where all goods are without duty.

Many Chinese articles are made here by factories moved from Shanghai, Canton.

Photo: Henri Cartier-Bresson (Magnum)

THERE ARE 7,000 PHILIPPINE ISLANDS

The Republic of the Philippines, given full independence on July 4, 1946, has some 7,110 islands, with over 4,500 of the smaller ones still unnamed. Discovered by Magellan in 1521, the Philippines for more than 300 years were part of Spain's vast empire, were ceded to the U.S. in 1898. Today, the new democracy has up-to-date facilities for tourists, welcomes them to its friendly, charming resorts.

Legaspi Landing, Manila Hotel: Damaged by war, the hotel is now fully restored.

Escolta Boulevard is one of the shopping streets of Manila, Philippines' big city.

Photos: Ewing Galloway

Rice terraces on Luzon (below) date back 1500 years, are still cultivated today.

University of Manila, badly bombed in war, has world's largest sun dial in garden.

Malacañan Palace in Manila is official residence of President of the Philippines.

Photos: Ewing Galloway; bottom right, Fenno Jacobs (Three Lions)

Temple of Dawn, in Bangkok, called *Wat Arun,* has 245-foot tower which gives a magnificent view of city from the top. It is surrounded by four smaller towers.

CLASSICAL DANCING IS ONE OF THE GLORIES OF SIAM'S HERITAGE.

THAILAND IS A NATION OF TEMPLES

There are few more entrancing sights in the world than the many temples of Siam, the country that's been known officially as Thailand since 1949. Bangkok, capital city, has many canals. Houses are often of teakwood, roofed with red tile. It is colorful city of almost a million people.

Photos: TWA Trans World Airline; bottom, Richard Joseph

Wat Po (wat means monastery or temple) is the most extensive in Bangkok and is noted for its reclining Buddha, with feet inlaid with designs of mother-of-pearl.

Wat Benchamaborpitr (Temple of the Fifth Sovereign) is built of Italian marble, Chinese tile, a combination of old Thai style with foreign materials, new methods.

JAKARTA, JAVA, IS INDONESIA CAPITAL

The Republic of Indonesia achieved its independence as recently as December 27, 1949. The island of Java, fourth largest of Indonesia group, is most important industrially, culturally, and politically.

Bandung is favorite vacation spot, 75 miles southeast of Jakarta, and with much more comfortable climate. This is Savoy-Homann Hotel, every room with balcony.

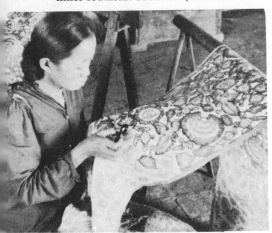

Java is noted for colorful and intricate batik, producing magnificent designs.

Native "taxis" wait for travelers coming from Jakarta's Tugu railway station.

Photos: Deane Dickason (Ewing Galloway); bottom left, Richard Joseph; bottom right, Owen (Black Star)

BALI IS SYMBOL OF THE FAR-AWAY

If you were asked to name the most exotic, far-away-from-it-all place you could think of, you might very well say "Bali"—the Indonesian island of batik, dancing girls, and good leisurely living.

Weaving is occupation of many Balinese women; they do colorful batik dye work.

Striking batik designs are used on the costumes used for the ceremonial dances.

Bali's predominant religion is Hinduism which spread to island in 7th century.

Women of Denpasar demonstrate the grace of carriage for which Balinese are known. Many go in for ritual dancing, wearing colorful costumes headdresses.

Photos: Richard Joseph

SUMATRA HAS MANY MOUNTAIN LAKES, LARGEST BEING LAKE TOBA.

SUMATRA COMPLETES INDONESIAN PICTURE

Sumatra is the second largest island of Indonesia. Java, Bali and Sumatra are the most important parts of the Indonesia group in terms of cultural development. There are major oil fields in Sumatra, and coal mines. The important cities of the island are Palembang, Medan, Padang.

Photo: Republic of Indo-
nesia Information Office

RANGOON MEANS "END OF STRIFE"

Originally a fishing village, Rangoon was won by King Alaungpaya, given its name to signalize his victory, and developed as the capital of Burma. Badly hit in World War II, it's now re-building.

The Independence Monument, Rangoon: Burma achieved independence in 1948.

Shwe Dagon Pagoda, 2 miles from center of Rangoon, is Buddha's greatest shrine.

Downtown Rangoon is dominated by the Sule Pagoda which enshrines a Hair of

Buddha and other Relics from India. At the right is the City Hall of Rangoon.

Singapore has regular taxis, but a more original way of getting about is in one of these "trishaws"—three-wheeled bicycles powered by sun-hatted drivers.

ANDERSON BRIDGE CROSSES SINGAPORE RIVER BY THE POST OFFICE.

SINGAPORE IS GATE TO THE FAR EAST

The British Colony of Singapore is the main port of call on route from Europe to the Far East, midway between India and China. Its famous Raffles Hotel has long been a symbol of the romance of world trade, and the Singapore sling a symbol of relaxation after work or play.

Photos: Horace Bristol (Black Star); bottom, Deane Dickason (Ewing Galloway)

Great Southern Hotel, Chinese-operated, has casement windows for maximum ventilation in the hot months. Beside hotel at left is Palace Theater, also Chinese.

Sultan Mohammed Mosque is on North Bridge Road, near Arab Street. One of the most beautiful sights in Singapore is the botanical garden with its monkey-jungle.

Photos: Deane Dickason (Ewing Galloway); bottom, Ewing Galloway

Clock-tower lighthouse is landmark in busy downtown Colombo, surrounded by a great variety of vehicles: native ox-carts, jinrickshas, modern motor cars.

PANORAMIC VIEW SHOWS HARBOR OF COLOMBO, CEYLON'S CAPITAL.

MUCH OF WORLD'S TEA COMES FROM CEYLON

Since 1948 Ceylon has been a dominion of the British Commonwealth. The capital city of Colombo has had many changes since World War I and is now one of the world's cleanest and most modern cities. Ceylon raises rice, coconuts, rubber, tea.

Photos: Deane Dickason (Ewing Galloway); bottom, Ewing Galloway

Golden Buddha in temple at Colombo:
Outside of town about 6 miles is the
Temple of Kelaniya, very sacred because
of a visit made to this spot by the Buddha.

The Perahera is an annual pageant held
in Kandy during the month of August.

Mount Lavinia Hotel, overlooking ocean,
is only eight miles outside of Colombo.

Photos: TWA Trans World Airline; Embassy
of Ceylon; Deane Dickason (Ewing Galloway)

411

INDIA IS LAND OF MYRIAD WONDERS

The Republic of India (a sovereign state since January 1950) boasts the famous Taj Mahal, sacred Ganges River, the great cities of Bombay, Calcutta, New Delhi, and the fabulous pink city of Jaipur.

The 20 ornate Jain temples in Calcutta are one of the city's great sights. Jainism is an offshoot of Hinduism, one belief being that it's wrong to kill, even insects.

412

Photo: TWA Trans World Airline

The Holy Ghat is bathing place in the Hooghly River (one of the many mouths of the Ganges) in Calcutta. Native "bum" boats provide transportation on river.

Calcutta's parks and gardens—Botanical, Zoological, Eden—have much of interest.

Belur Temple, eight miles from Calcutta, is center of Shri Ramakrishna Mission.

Photos: Alice Schalek (Three Lions); Richard Joseph; Government of India Tourist Office

View of the Himalayas (which in Sanskrit means "abode of snow") from Sandakphu. Conquest of Everest and Annapurna has drawn world interest in this great range.

The Bathing Ghats and temples on bank of the Ganges River are visited by tens of thousands each year. Hindus come to the sacred river as Moslems go to Mecca.

New Delhi, seat of the government of the Republic of India, is a magnificent city.

Picturesque old buildings mingle with modern ones. This is President's house.

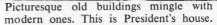

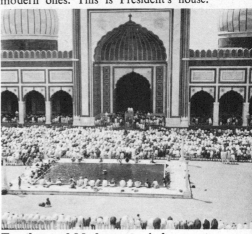

Group of round-the-world tourists finds elephant ride the oddest transportation.

Ten thousand Moslems pray before great Mosque of Delhi on a Friday morning.

Sikh taxi drivers of Calcutta don't look like their New York or Chicago brethren.

Jantar Mantar is early 18th-century observatory constructed by a Rajput King.

Photos: Richard Joseph; top, Deane Dickason (Ewing Galloway); center right, Ewing Galloway

The Taj Mahal, made entirely of white marble, is a world famed masterpiece. It was built 1630–48, at Agra, by Shah Jehan as memorial to his beloved wife.

Panch Mahal is one of ornate buildings at fabulous deserted city of Fatehpur Sikri, about 20 miles from Agra. City was abandoned because of lack of water.

Photos: Deane Dickason (Ewing Galloway); bottom, Richard Joseph

From Malabar Hill in Bombay, you look down on the Marine Drive and Chow- patty Beach, favorite place for meetings, walking, good spot to observe people.

Bombay's Silk Bazaar is a bustling row of shops, wholesale and retail. One of most interesting shopping areas for the foreigner is Crawford Market section.

Photos: TWA Trans World Air- line; bottom, Ewing Galloway

417

Temple of Neminath is largest of the numerous Jain temples on Mount Girnar, a nearly circular mountain which has been sacred since before the Christian Era.

Great Temple at Rameswaram, on island in South India, is much venerated shrine.

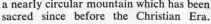

Barber in Calcutta does not require a shop, simply plies his trade on sidewalk.

Indian types at Darjeeling market; from here you can watch sunrise over Everest.

418

Photos: Deane Dickason (Ewing Galloway); center right and bottom right, Richard Joseph

VALE OF KASHMIR IS A GARDEN SPOT

Kashmir is one of the loveliest countries of the East, traversed by lofty ranges of the Himalayas, with lakes, rivers, forests. It is noted for its rich agriculture and its manufactures, especially Cashmeres.

Srinagar, capital of Kashmir, on the Jhelum River, is known as "Venice of the East," intersected with canals and waterways, with boats as transportation.

Dal Lake, on outskirts of Srinagar, has several Moghul Gardens, visited by boat.

A shikara, a sort of Kashmiri gondola, takes you about in canalled Srinagar.

Hyderabad, one of main cities of Western Pakistan, has its own style of air-conditioning: wind scoops on most of the buildings take in air, force it downward.

PAKISTAN IS DIVIDED INTO TWO REGIONS

Pakistan, once a province of India, was made an independent state in 1947, as a homeland for Indian Moslems. The two parts of the nation are separated by 900 miles of Indian territory. The larger part is West Pakistan, with Karachi as its capital. East Pakistan, one-sixth as large, has as its regional capital, Dacca.

Balconies are characteristic of houses in Karachi. While auto traffic grows, the victorias still thrive.

Photos: Deane Dickason (Ewing Galloway); bottom, Camera Clix

Human-headed Sphinx guards 3 Pyramids of Giza. At left is Pyramid of Khafra.

Near Great Pyramid, Kamal el-Malakh made his discovery of the Cheops bark.

"Look, no hands!" say camel-mounted nomads, eager for a piaster or two.

EGYPT IS ANCIENT LAND OF THE NILE

The origin of Egypt's hoary culture is not revealed even in the many writings that have come down to us in all sorts of early forms. Some findings of the Ancient Kingdom date as far back as 3400 B.C., and the greatest creative period was from about 1580 to 945 B.C. Today you can ride in air-conditioned trains, stay in comfort at the Semiramis Hotel on the Nile (which has taken the place of burned-down Shepheard's), or at Mena House in shadow of pyramids.

Photos: TWA Trans World Airline, bottom, Richard Joseph

Egypt

The great Citadel in Cairo was built about 1179 by Saladin. It contains the beautiful Mosque of Mohammed Ali, with its alabaster walls, myriad lamps.

Cairo bazaars offer brass goods, marble and alabaster, gold and silver inlays.

Nile boat is shown opposite Cataract hotel at Aswan, site of irrigation dam.

Egyptian women of Luxor, the ancient city of Thebes, use their heads to help their hands when there are burdens to carry. Tomb of Tut-ankh-amen is here.

Egyptian wall paintings, still remarkably bright, decorate wall of King Tut's tomb.

Alabaster Sphinx is one of sights at Memphis, capital of the Old Kingdom.

Temple of Luxor, built 1400 B.C., has huge pillars over fifty feet in height.

Photos: Henri Cartier-Bresson (Magnum); center left, TWA Trans World Airline; bottom left, S. A. Booth; bottom right, Egyptian State Tourist Office

ADVENTURE CALLS IN BRITISH EAST AFRICA

Whether your name is Hemingway or Smith, you'll find East Africa a land of great variety, abundant wild life, amazing flora. It has the highest mountain (Kilimanjaro) and the largest lake (Victoria) on the continent. British East Africa consists of the Colony and Protectorate of Kenya, Protectorates of Uganda, Zanzibar, Trust Territory of Tanganyika.

Uganda woman and child: The Baganda are a very advanced, progressive people.

Newly initiated Masai warriors: They come from independent fighting tribe.

Dar es Salaam, meaning "Haven of Peace," is the capital of Tanganyika Territory. This harbor, almost landlocked, handles over half of territory's exports.

Two full-maned lions seek the shade of a tree on Serengeti Plains, Tanganyika.

Arab dhows have traded with the East African coast for at least ten centuries.

Photos: East Africa Railways & Harbours; top right, lower left, Tanganyika Public Relations Dept.; bottom right, Len Young

Elephants and other big game abound in the Amboseli Game Reserve lying below

Africa's highest mountain—the snow-capped dome of Kilimanjaro, 19,340 ft.

Mt. Kenya is 17,056 ft. high. Some of Kenya tribes think it residence of gods.

Kilindini harbor on Mombasa Island is the gateway to both Kenya and Uganda.

Photos: Len Young; bottom right,
East Africa Railways & Harbours

VICTORIA FALLS SURPASSES NIAGARA IN BOTH WIDTH AND HEIGHT.

DAVID LIVINGSTONE EXPLORED RHODESIA

British influence in Northern and Southern Rhodesia owes much to Livingstone and to Cecil Rhodes. Southern Rhodesia is in new Central African Federation which also includes Northern Rhodesia and Nyasaland. Victoria Falls, greatest natural feature of area, is on border between Northern and Southern Rhodesia.

426

SOUTH AFRICA IS LAND OF CONTRASTS

Union of South Africa, British dominion of 13 million people, has busy cities of Johannesburg, Cape Town and Durban, fabulous gold mines, the great Kruger National Park, endless stretches of veld.

Johannesburg's busy Commissioner Street shows mushroom growth of gold center.

Drakensberg mountains tower above tourist hostel in Natal National Park.

Pretoria is the Union's administrative capital, though the legislature convenes

at Cape Town. Winston Churchill escaped from prison here during Boer War, 1899.

427

Union of South Africa

Durban is magnificently located on Natal Bay of the Indian Ocean. Marine Parade has many fine hotels. There is wonderful surf, lake fishing, with unique ski-boats.

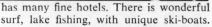

Visit to Kruger National Park is thrilling. You stay in thatched cottages, cook meals outdoors if you like. You drive right by lions, zebras, leopards, hippos!

Photos: South Africa Tourist Corporation; Pan American World Airways; South African Railways

Kimberley diamond mine reached 1,200 feet as open mine; shafts were carried to 4,000 feet. This mine was abandoned in 1915, but area is still diamond center.

In Durban, you see Zulus in gay costume and headdress drawing rickshas in street.

All these diamonds came from one day's output of Wesselton, Dutoitspan mines.

Union of South Africa

Cape Town, legislative capital of the Union, has many impressive buildings.

Flower Market is in front of City Hall, with Table Mountain in background.

Aerial cableway to top of Table Mountain, 3,500 feet, gives view of both

Atlantic and Indian Oceans. Cape Town has lovely harbor, is compared to Naples.

Photos: Pan American World Airways

Voyage 10
SOUTH PACIFIC

World War II opened up new interest in the South Pacific for thousands of Americans. You may never have been nearer than reading *Tales of the South Pacific* by James Michener, or seeing the great musical show based on it, but you have an idea of its romance, and the vigor of the great frontier lands, Australia and New Zealand.

Here's a typical flight by Pan American: You leave San Francisco a minute before midnight. At 6:45 in the morning, Honolulu time, you are in the Hawaiian islands for a brief rest. You leave at noon and arrive at Canton Island 7:45 p.m. Between there and Suva in the Fiji Islands, you cross the International Date Line and lose a day! If you've left San Francisco at midnight Sunday, you arrive at Suva's Nandi Airport at 12:01 a.m. Wednesday. For New Zealand, you take off an hour later, at 1:00, and are in Auckland at 8:15 p.m. If you are headed for Australia, you leave Nandi at 1:30 a.m. and arrive at Sydney at 8:00 p.m.

From London, BOAC and Qantas (the Australian Government-owned airline) run flights by way of Cairo, Karachi and Singapore. From Vancouver, you take Canadian Pacific or Qantas Empire Airways. And between Australia,

Pan American "Clipper" heads west.

New Zealand and Fiji there is service by TEAL'S DC6's.

Good ship service from North America is now provided by the Orient Line. If you have plenty of time, there are freighters that plod their leisurely way across the Pacific, some from New York by way of the Panama Canal. From London, several liners make the trip via the Suez canal in less than a month. Others go around Africa and take thirty to forty-five days, calling en route at Madeira or one of the Canary Islands, Cape Town and Durban.

Within Australia, there's good transportation by railways, air services, and busses. Distances are not as great in New Zealand which is about as big as New York and Illinois combined. Renting a car is good way to see all of its beauties.

Photo: Pan American World Airways

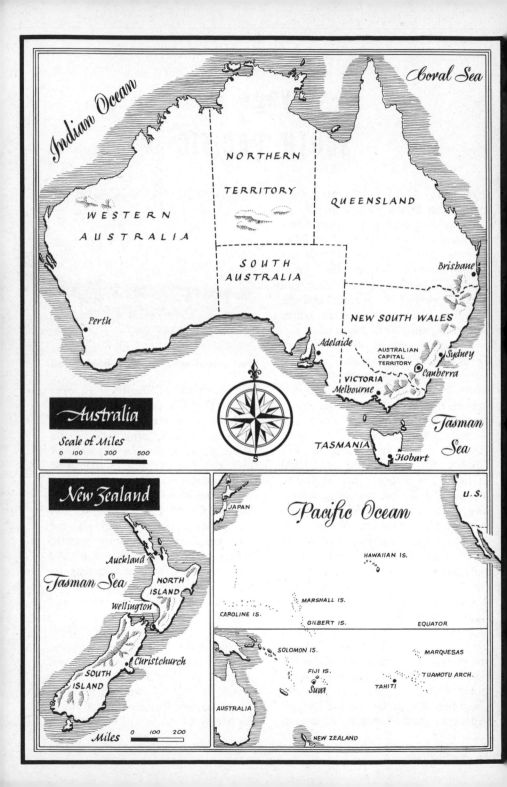

FIJI'S 250 ISLANDS ARE TROPIC HEAVEN

Most important British colony in Pacific, the Fiji Islands are 2500 miles southwest of Hawaii. Some say there are 250 isles, others up to 320. 80 are inhabited. The largest is Viti Levu, with capital of Suva.

Natives of Suva were once cruel cannibals; converting them was a religious triumph. Population is now about 40% Fijian, 50% Indian and 10% other races.

Grand Pacific Hotel in Suva is one of the best known Pacific hostelries. It entertained during the war hundreds of U.S., British, and other Allied officers.

Photos: Ewing Galloway; bottom, Rob Wright (Black Star)

DOMINATED BY ITS GREAT BRIDGE OVER AN ARM OF THE HARBOR, SYDI

AUSTRALIA IS BIG
AS UNITED STATES

The smallest of the continents, Australia is still very nearly as large in area as the United States—but it has only about nine million inhabitants. Known as "the sunshine continent," it is a land where you can live outdoors much of the time, with such sports as golf, skiing, fishing, bathing on wonderful beaches.

Photo: Pan American World Airways

Eighteen footers take part in yachting regatta in beautiful harbor of Sydney.

"LEASURE CITY OF THE SOUTH SEAS."

Sydney is the largest city, with over a million and a half population. Other principal cities are Brisbane, Melbourne, Adelaide, Perth, and Hobart on island of Tasmania, lying to the south, 150 miles from Melbourne. Australia, up-and-coming British dominion, has a vitality and an optimism that appeal to Americans.

Canberra is federal capital of Australia, with Parliament House, lovely gardens.

Photos: Australian National Publicity Association; Australian News and Information Bureau

Melbourne from bank of the Yarra River: Australia's second largest city lies at the head of Port Phillip Bay, an almost land-locked inlet just over 30 miles long.

There's good fishing for trout in mountain streams and in spillways of big dams.

Riding is popular in Melbourne, and city has the Melbourne Cup race each fall.

Photos: Australian National Publicity Association

In Melbourne's trim Fitzroy Gardens is cottage in which Captain Cook lived.

Skiiers find new chalets at Mt. Hotham (above), Mt. Buffalo, Mt. Kosciusko.

Hobart, capital of island of Tasmania, lies at the foot of Mt. Wellington. It has swinging bridge across Derwent River, with a floating portion 3,168 feet long.

Photos: Australian National-al Publicity Association

Australia

The Great Barrier Reef extends over 1,200 miles along the Queensland coast.

Australian bushland is world-famous for its dense growth of trees, ferns, flowers.

Cattle crossing at river in Queensland: Dairy cattle are raised in the richer coastal areas, and much beef is raised for local use and for export to England.

Photos: Australian National · Publicity Association

Flowering trees of Brisbane frame its City Hall. Brisbane is capital of the pastoral state of Queensland with its coastal plantations of fruit, sugar cane.

The wattle, with pale-golden blossoms, is Australia's national tree and flower.

Koala Bears are easily tamed, perfectly harmless, feed exclusively on eucalyptus.

Photos: Australian National Publicity Association; bottom right, Pan American World Airways

Australia

Perth, capital of Western Australia, is on the Swan River, about 12 miles from port city of Fremantle. King's Park is a thousand acres of natural bushland.

Macdonnell Ranges in central Australia have odd formation, as though fashioned by giants. Town of Alice Springs, in mountains, has grown much in 10 years.

x

440

Photos: Australian National Publicity Association

Ant Hill in Northern Territory: There are many square miles of rugged country.

Northern Territory still has many of the aboriginal tribes, like these fishermen.

Adelaide, South Australia's capital, is a well planned city, rich in parks and gardens. It is near the great Gulf St. Vincent, 90 miles long, 45 miles across.

Photos: Australian National-
al   Publicity   Association

NEW ZEALAND HAS MATCHLESS BEAUTY

New Zealand is a wonderland of scenery: The Southern Alps have over 200 peaks of 7,500 feet and more, with Mount Cook rising to 12,349. There are lakes and waterfalls, fertile farms and bushland.

Wellington, capital of the Dominion, is built on steep hills about a magnificent harbor, 3 miles wide and 12 long. The hills are climbed by trams, cable cars reminiscent of those in San Francisco.

Rotorua is center of Maori life, with wonderful carvings; also has thermal spa.

Wanganui River runs through primeval forest in beautiful thermal wonderland.

New Zealand

Auckland, built on the shores of deeply indented Waitemata harbor, is chief port and largest city of New Zealand. This is view of the north shore from Mount Eden.

Wellington has tunnels that take roads, trolley lines through encircling hills.

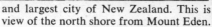

University Tower, Auckland: Nation is proud of education, social legislation.

Photos: New Zealand Government;
Three Lions; Ewing Galloway

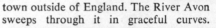

Christchurch, the largest city on South Island, is the most typically English town outside of England. The River Avon sweeps through it in graceful curves.

Sutherland Falls, 1,904 feet high, is one of world's tallest, most beautiful.

Pohutu Geyser is one of many in the Hot Springs district health resort, Rotorua.

GAUGUIN DID MANY PAINTINGS IN SOUTH SEA PARADISE OF TAHITI.

TAHITI IS THE END
OF OUR WORLD TOUR

Kon-Tiki brought home to thousands of readers the lure of primitive life in the South Seas, and especially the tiny islands of Polynesia. Queen of them all in the dreams of men is Tahiti, supreme symbol of living for the simple joy of living . . . a good place to end our trip.